MY JOURNEY
in His Hands

BETTY L. CAMPBELL
Edited by Tammy Moore

Edited by Tammy Moore
Book design by YellowStudios
Cover photography by Gochenour Photography
Author headshot by Brubaker Photography
Hair design by Kimberly Smith at Aranda Salon

Paperback ISBN: 978-1-7378121-1-1
Library of Congress Control Number: *pending*

Printed in the United States of America

To Charlise and Velvet...

Foreword

Betty's journey to Christ and with Christ is a story every-one should read. All of us feel like our lives don't matter from time to time, we wonder why certain things happen to us, and we grieve the decisions we could have made better in this life. But Betty's story gives all of us hope.

God's not done with you and God's not done with Betty and her story. Through the trials and temptations Jesus Christ met her at every turn. God used the pain of Betty's life to instill in her the passion she now has to love people whom everyone else has forgotten. She is taking the Gos-pel to where people need it most, like Jesus did in his day.

I came in contact with Betty through her husband Tony who used to be a part of our church in Colorado Springs, Vanguard Church. It is amazing to see how God ordered Betty and Tony's steps to intersect at this season of their lives and live out this gigantic calling He has placed on their shoulders. I am honored to know them and even more so honored to be a part of this book project to spread the word about Xpose Hope Ministries.

Maybe you yourself are in a dark place in your life, maybe you have been dislodged and disillusioned by the pain and sorrow of your life story. Maybe you, like Betty at one point, have lost the will to live and think the world would be a better place without you. Maybe you don't think God can redeem your story and the suffering you have grown through and even caused yourself. If so, you need to read Betty's journey. She will help you pick your soul up off the dark cold floor of this life and breathe new life and hope back into you. You don't have to be ashamed of your story. You don't have to have all the answers to be used by God. You don't have to make sense of everything, you just need to say to the Lord Jesus like Betty, "Use me Lord for your glory."

There is a whole world of people out there who desperately need to hear and experience the love of Jesus Christ. I pray you let Betty's story inspire you as it has me. I laughed, cried, wept, and thanked Jesus through this book, that in my lowest darkest moments He never left me like He never left Betty. I see the fingerprints of God on my life by reading Betty's story and I believe you will too.

Don't give up, give in, or give out on the calling God has placed on your life

Get up and get going again.

If you have a pulse, you still have a Divine purpose for being here right now on planet earth. Fight through the trauma, the drama, the criticism, the opposition and say to the Lord like Isaiah did, like Betty does in this book, "Here am I Lord, Send me! Send me and spend me, I give you my all!"

May you be inspired as I was by Betty's journey and may we all one day arrive at the same place, at the feet of Jesus worshipping Him in heaven as the King of Kings and Lord of Lords. Until then, let's Xpose Hope for others who need to hear and experience the love of Jesus Christ.

Blessings,
Pastor Kelly M. Williams
Senior Pastor
Vanguard Church
Colorado Springs, CO

Acknowledgements

This book began more than a decade ago. The name was the name of our cancer blog. My husband, Layne, believed that people needed to know that even with cancer one could find hope. As my life turned into new chapters, I came to the realization that life is not so much about a destination as it is about the journey. Even more, is the lesson to trust and lean more and more on Jesus who walks with me every step on this path called "my life." He walked with me when life was beautiful and He held me when I was enveloped in darkness.

I needed a new script to help me trust when I don't understand. The lessons in this life are continuous opportunities to learn to be joyful in hard times, and cloaked in peace in the unseen storms that I have yet to face. At some point, I opened my hand and asked Him to take pen I'd been clinging to. "Jesus, will you please take this and rewrite my story to the end?"

A book like this doesn't happen without all the people who supported me and encouraged me to write it. However, because it is about my life, I feel proud to honor some of the wonderful people who changed my life. I'm sure I am missing many, but not because they were not important.

I want to acknowledge first, Jesus my Savior, who held me close through the crazy up and down rollercoaster of my life. He held me, even when I fought Him.

I wouldn't be who I am without my family; my siblings, my loving parents, Aunt Betty and Uncle Ray who ensured that I knew Christ. I give heartfelt love and gratitude for Layne who was my constant companion and soulmate. You were the spouse with whom I grew up, and learned about life and I ever cherish my memories of us together. You taught me to love the unlovable. Through your life, I saw what true worship looked like.

To Tony. You are my adoring second chapter, who was willing to walk into a path we could not easily distinguish, demonstrating sacrificial love. I am inspired by your bravery to stand for what is right, especially when it would have been easy to walk away.

To my children, who have seen me at my best and at my worst; you are each precious to me, though we may not always agree. I am proud of each of you! You are my legacy to the world.

And of course, my first real church home and to all those at Washington Avenue United Methodist Church, and

Stoutsville Camp. The youth who attended, every pastor and camp administrator who helped to mold and change my life. Special thanks to those daring youth pastors, who undoubtedly shook their heads and rolled their eyes at my antics.

My fourth-grade teacher, Mrs. Boggs. I felt lonely and lost, but you tenderly carried me through heavy sorrow after the death of my mom. You made me feel less out of place.

I must acknowledge the many doctors who cared for my husband, oncologists, surgeons, readiologists. All amazing and all surrounding us with hope. I need to especially thank Dr. Nutting in Colorado, you are an amazing man of God, and surgeon. My dear friend Melissa my nurse, who came and gave me a time of rest. For all doctors, nurses, volunteers and staff who have dedicated their lives to help save patients and comfort families who are fighting for their lives, I thank you.

My close friend Connie, who opened her door to me immediately. reminded me that this was not fair, and your humor and sarcasm always brought a bring a smile to my face.

Norris and Betty, always on mission. And of course, Ginger and Tim, and the others who walked the EC path with me.

Tim and Lori who didn't turn their backs when Layne died, and still stand watch over my family.

The counselors at the Washington County Domestic Violence Resource Center. Angels in plain clothing, they are! They helped me, and now they assist my clients.

My fabulous surgeon, Dr. Corey Vandezandschulp. Because of him, I walk today. Thanks to the entire staff and wonderful volunteers of Providence Legacy Hospital. I cannot forget the unknown nurse at St. Vincent's Hospital, whose name I don't recall, who helped me navigate the system, found me a piano to play and showed me the path to healing.

My entire Honda ST group at WeSToc. I will never forget your kindness during my grief. My dear friend, Tony Mills, who held me up when life was too hard. Thanks for reminding me that my home, though far away, is always with me.

Thank you to Lynda and Dave. When I have felt like I could not face one more sad story, you gave me a "secret" getaway retreat near the crashing waves, sand dollars, and osprey at the coast. Without your kindness, this book would not exist.

Thank you to Patta, the owner of the Sea Café in Astoria, for allowing me to steal the corner booth in a comfy chair sipping mint tea, while watching ships out of the corner of my eye gliding through the harbor for many a long hour. It was the perfect writer's nook. I highly suggest it!

I must acknowledge Leslie, Katie, and Patty, the first strong and courageous women to follow me, bringing light into the darkness along with me. I am delighted with the entire team at Xpose Hope, including those who have since moved on, and those who are yet to come. I am grateful for our connected churches and service agencies. Thank you too, our Bend, Pasco County and Great Falls teams and every business that supports Xpose Hope in big ways and small. You mean so much to me!

To my amazing editor, Tammy Moore, an amazing woman who kept my voice strong, even in the portions of this book that were very difficult for me to write. A wild mustang she is...that should never be staked to a pole and put on a carrousel. She needs to run free as God made her.

To my coach and friend Darcey Edwards. Thank you for pushing me forward with your message of resilience to never to give up, and to remind me of who God made me to be. Thanks for always having my back.

To coach Richard Zelke, who helped me focus on my "why."

To the first woman that we ever lost, Kim. A sprite of a woman, she brought joy everywhere she went. I have not forgotten you...a piece of you is embedded deep in my soul. I'm sorry that there wasn't more we could do. I pray you are in God's arms now.

To Charlise and Velvet, and the others I left behind in the life. I pray that you also have found a light on your path for your journey in His hands.

And finally, to every woman affected by the adult industry--may you know that God loves you. You are cherished and adored! He seeks for you to know Him.

Author's Note

It took me some time to write this story, because it took me some time to tell my entire family, including my children, about my past. I understand the need for privacy in that respect. Therefore, most names and locations have been changed to allow those in my life the privacy of their own journey. There are no villains in this story.

For God so loved the world, that He gave his only begotten son, that whosoever believeth on him might be saved. Even those with whom we disagree, or who are no longer in our lives.

Every person written about herein, is indeed, a beloved child of the King.

—Betty L. Campbell

It took a lot of courage to take a journey back in time to cross that threshold and to pierce into the darkness— back into a world from long ago. Thumping bass beats greeted us in the dimly lit, burgundy embellished room. A woman crouched down spread eagle on stage bathed in light caught my attention.

"Well, I just lost Katie. I'm pretty sure about that," the thought was nearly audible.

We made our way back to the dressing room. A dressing room not unlike the one of my youth, where I had sold my very soul in an attempt to be someone to myself, my husband and to men I didn't even know. In every woman, I saw myself. Young, thin, makeup ladened and hollow.

After 30 years, I was home. And I could finally give love....to myself.

I didn't begin life on a stripper pole and I didn't dream of the idea when I was 8. I played "school" with my friends, assigning tasks and graded pretend papers with red ink. I was a princess who went on lavish pretend dates with imaginary boys, escorted in luxury to royal balls. I was a normal child...well, as normal as could be expected considering the trauma I'd endured in my life. So, how did the life of the executive director of a nonprofit, reaching those in the trafficking and sex industry with the message of hope, begin?

It was winter of 1968. What I pulled from my closet to wear, I can't remember, but what *she* wore is still etched in my mind. Monique was one of the girls from my school, one of my classmates. Mom and Dad let me stay up late to attend the basketball game that night, just long enough to see the larger-than-life queen's court. Her Cinderella styled dress sparkled in the spotlights. She wore a silver tiara and her brunette hair bounced in tight spiral curls that draped gracefully down her back. Everything matched and glistened from her jewelry right down to the shoes.

After the ceremony, my parents took me home and tucked me into bed. For them, however, the night was only beginning.

My parents stood by, waiting for the phone to ring. My 15-year-old brother, Michael and 13-year-old sister would soon be calling for them to pick them up as soon as the game was over. He was in charge of the concession stand, and it was running low on popcorn. He made a decision that would change our family forever. He decided to break a rule. We were given strict orders to never get into vehicles with other teens. The drive to Kelley's market to grab a few bags of popcorn would only take a few minutes; short, fast and under Mom and Dad's radar. Michael probably could have dashed over on foot faster than driving, but instead, just this one time, he piled into a vehicle with two other boys.

They never saw the train that hit them. Dusk had nearly faded to dark, and the locomotive, inexplicably, had no lights, and never blew its horn. There was no crossing arm. Although my brother's only injury was a broken nose, he slipped into shock. Despite the valiant efforts from the volunteer medics at the local fire department, he never made it to the hospital, and that night... I learned about death.

I didn't understand death, and in my innocence and naivety, the next day, I shared in my first-grade class of my brother's death, in of all things—show and tell. My teacher put her hand to her mouth, frozen for a moment before putting on a smile and quickly going to the next student. She spoke with a wise calmness that I could only appreciate later as an adult, looking back.

Mom was never really the same after that night. She had suffered multiple miscarriages before conceiving my brother, and his death ripped a piece of her heart away that would never heal. I was too young to understand why, but I knew that sadness permeated our home like a heavy, damp blanket.

Mom's emphysema grew worse and worse, and before too long, she was carrying a portable oxygen tank everywhere she went. Eventually, we moved an electric hospital bed into our family room. Sitting with Mom on her bed while she brushed my hair, watching Gunsmoke became as normal to me as it was to sit with dad in his recliner. I never questioned the box filled with prescription medications or the hole drilled in the wall which ran oxygen tubes from large tanks in the garage. I had no idea we could no longer enjoy the warmth and ambiance of fires in the fireplace due to the use of oxygen in the room.

It was my new normal. I adjusted. It's what we do.

There, next to the fireplace, was my mom's hospital bed. She had been staying there since she was put on oxygen. In those days, there were no automatic oxygen pumps and the big tanks were too dangerous and heavy to be taken into the house.

Nearly three years had come and gone since Michael's funeral. My mom and dad had changed since then. Their voices, quiet and subdued. The laughter and brother-sister banter died along with Michael. The house itself, as though it had a soul, felt cold, empty and solemn. Mom's health faded. Our family camping trips which encompassed most of our summer months came to a halt.

We still canned from the garden, but it was my sister, who did most of the preparation. Gone, were the days when friends spent hours on the back porch, breaking green beans into pots while chatting about the news, or what relative had gout.

On my ninth birthday, I had a small party in the family room. Mom sat on the edge of her bed and I turned to show her each gift as I opened it, while Dad snapped photos. We ate a sheet birthday cake which my sister had baked. I tore open a present from one of my friend's brother. That moment my spirit seemed to float with glee as I gazed on a pair of plastic high heels. "Oh my! I must be grown up now to be gifted such a set of shoes," I mused. The lines between reality and fantasy blurred together, undefined, and I felt a happiness that seemed to pull me, in that moment, out of my gray world, void of color.

It didn't seem odd to me that my mom slept downstairs, and my father slept in their room upstairs. I assumed everyone's parents lived like this, and I expected that as soon as mom began to feel better, she'd move back upstairs. Right now, though, climbing the stairs was an arduous chore that left her winded and exhausted.

I hated mornings. This was an ordinary school day like any other. "Betty Lou...time to get up!" I pushed back the blankets, stumbled out of bed, trotted downstairs, and shoveled down a bowl of cereal for breakfast. The spoon and bowl clattered as I dropped them into the sink before I pulled my lunch money from a container in a drawer. I scurried back up the stairs to the bathroom to brush my teeth and pull a comb through my hair. Mom and Aunt Carol cut it into a cute little pixie cut so I could take care of it myself.

I slid on my favorite orange and black checkered tent dress, complete with a giant white Peter Pan collar. Far from being fashionable, it was my comfortable go-to outfit that I loved to twirl around in. Lastly, I'd tug up my knee socks, and tie my shoes. "The rabbit goes around the tree and in the hole, then you pull his ears," I'd remind myself, giggling at the funny story my parents told me to help me remember the process.

I grabbed my books, and stuffed my homework papers inside, before bouncing back down the stairs to the dining room, around the banister, then down a second set to the family room. Every morning, like this one included a race to get to Mom before my little brother. I liked being the first one to get a kiss and hug before we went to the neighbor's driveway to catch our school bus.

I could see her lying on the hospital bed and heard the hissssss of the oxygen being sprayed into her nostrils as I reached the bottom of the stairway. This morning was so quiet. "Oh," I thought, "Mom must still be sleeping. Well, I could still get the first kiss in on her cheek."

I leaned over and kissed her on her cheek. She was cold to my lips. I held her hands. They were hard, and cold. "Mom?" I whispered in a panic. I gently shook her shoulder. "Mom! Wake up!... Mom?" Noooo.

My mind flashed to one of my dad's western tv shows, thinking, "this is just like Gunsmoke." She was not fighting to breathe and her chest was still. I pressed my ear against her chest. Silence. Mom was dead.

Everything changed in that moment. All my childhood dreams were swept to the side. As I faced seeing my mother gone, looking death in the face, I now needed to be a big girl. I had to tell someone and I instinctively knew that I needed to protect my five-year-old brother who too little to understand.

I marched upstairs and stood in front of Mom's helper. "Mom is dead," I announced in a matter-of-fact voice.

She shook her head and admonished me, "That isn't a thing to kid about!" Her loud sobs began as she descended down the stairs. I didn't cry. I didn't have any emotion.

My father sent us to school that day, so he could handle having Mom's body removed and make funeral arrangements. No autopsy was done since she had been under medical care. Her death was listed as resulting from her disease. That much was true. But it wasn't a "natural" death. I wouldn't learn until I was an adult that my mother had, in fact, committed suicide.

My class was doing testing that day in the cafeteria. My teacher suggested that I sit out. I didn't want to be different than all the other kids. I took my state tests, and I quietly wondered—how should a girl without a mom act?

The letter she left indicated she felt like she was impacting her children's lives negatively. Once she needed oxygen all the time, she took the blame upon herself for ending our summer camping adventures. Because she tired so easily, she realized it would be impossible to be the mom who was able cut our sandwiches diagonally, or as we called it "school-ways." She couldn't easily make our dinners, or give us perms; the hairstyle of the day. Climbing the stairs to and from the basement to do laundry was just too much. She decided that her existence contributed nothing to the family. Filled with guilt, she believed that she had become a heavy weight and a burden—one that she no longer could bear watching us to carry.

From this, I learned that a good mother gives everything to her children, including her own life, if necessary.

Many kids grow up before experiencing death with a close family member or loved one, commenced with the final ceremony; the funeral. This was my third one in three years. Not only did we lose Michael in his teen years, my dad's brother had passed only months before. Funeral homes, flowers, family coming to pay respects and bring food to the house... that was all normal. Our sad, quiet home was soaked in more tears and awkward silence. However, an incident at the visitation services changed my life.

Our family was Catholic. My mother converted when she married my father and she was an ardent convert. To say we were active in the church would be an understatement. We were baptized at three days old. We all celebrated our first communions, our first confessions and we attended catechism. We know my father's birthdate, not because of a birth record, but because he was baptized in the Catholic church in Slovenia.

One evening, some nuns arrived at the funeral home. They seemed to me to be very upset over my mother's passing. What I didn't know was they were inebriated.

Drunk as skunks. One was draped across the casket. Dad was livid. He muttered in a quiet rage, that he would never, ever enter the doors of a church again. After the funeral, as far as I know, he kept that vow. He dropped us off at the church for our religious classes, but he never attended another service that I can remember.

My church upbringing then fell to my Aunt Betty and Uncle Ray on my mother's side. They were members of an Evangelical United Brethren (EUB) church that was changed to a United Methodist when the Methodists chose to combine with the EUB denomination. It was at this small church in South Columbus that I first began to have a real relationship with Jesus. I loved the Sunday School classes, the youth group, and was so excited to attend Stoutsville Camp when I was a teenager. All the kids were talking about it.

The camp had a wooden tabernacle that was basically a barn with sides that tilted outward, propped up by sticks to let the breeze flow through. The pews and altar were roughhewn and it had a raised area for speakers. It was at this painted wood altar that I had my first real conversation with Jesus, as everyone sang the hymn, "I Surrender All." The speaker was John Maxwell, who at the time was merely the pastor of a single church. He later came to our church to educate us on how to do bus ministry. Imagine my shock when I returned to my faith in

Christ, walking into a Christian bookstore and seeing a "John Maxwell Bible."

From the moment my mother died, in a moment, I went from being like everyone else, to being the little girl who doesn't have a mom. People meant well, but I heard the whispers. When I was in Little League cheerleading, the moms had a conversation about our uniforms. The mothers always sewed these.

"But who will sew Betty Lou's?"

"I believe her sister sews."

And so it was that my sister became my back-up mom. She and Aunt Betty did their best to fill in at mother-daughter banquets, bra fittings, and other coming of age events.

I remember clearly, my sister attempting to give me "the talk" in our camper. I found this so strange that I just got up and left. I would garner the information on the facts of life from friends. Those were the 70's and more than a decade away from the age of the internet. Much of what I heard was far from correct, but I faked my way through when the time came.

I lived in a small town in Ohio, and everyone knew everyone's business, including mine. Later, when attending my aunt's church in Columbus, my story, of course followed me. I knew that everyone realized I was orphaned, from their sad glances and condescending behaviors. I hated being different. Life was unfair and I wished I could be like everyone else.

I only felt comfortable being around two friends. One was Becky. Her grandmother played piano at church and she also ran the children's church. Her mother left her to be raised by her grandmother, so she was also different. Then, there was John. John was the product of a divorced family, who suffered at the hands of a verbally and physically abusive stepfather. Those were times when blended families were almost unheard of. When the three of us were together, we were our own kind of normal.

My aunt's church sent their youth to a rustic old -time summer camp. Older adults were resident care takers who enjoyed living in the peaceful, country cabins. Our church had two cabins, and next door, were the kids from the Chillicothe United Methodist church. Needless to say, many summer time romances bloomed between those two cabins.

One of the big highlights of the camp was a formal dinner on the last Friday of camp. The girls put on pretty dresses and the boys sported nice suits. I never managed to come up with a date. One year, one of the well-meaning girls in my cabin felt so sorry for me that she paid a young man to take me to the dinner. I was elated, until he told me that he was returning the money. He'd had a great time and told me that he didn't have to be paid to take me out.

Though he and I dated for two years after that, I never forgot that I was the girl who had to have a date purchased for her. I still was different. I didn't fit in.

A small line of teens stretched outside our pastor's office. Our church required that a young person attain their approval in order to attend one of the denomination colleges.

One thing I knew for sure. I belonged there. In fact, I felt pretty pompous about it. I'd heard God talk to me in the prayer room under the tabernacle at Stoutsville. I clearly heard him telling me that He was calling me into ministry. For once in my life, it didn't matter if I was the odd man out. Who— after all, could stand in my way if the God who spoke the universe and creation into being, in six days had ordained me for His purpose? I imagined myself in the pulpit, expounding the Word to a crowd. I envisioned the people responding to an altar call, coming forward. I could hear the music. Maybe I would be asked to go to China. I was so excited to spend my life with God, who would not leave me.... or die on me.

Preparation was exciting! I'd spent the entire year eating up every theology book I could get my hands on, including shelves filled with books of Uncle Ray's large collection. I treated the books as a treasure trove of vast wealth. Out of respect for Uncle Ray and the writings, I was careful not to make any marks or fold the corners, returning them in perfect condition so I could borrow more. I had devoured more than 500 theological texts during my time at their home.

Besides knowing I had a great call on my life, my Aunt Betty was the chair of the church board. I was a shoe-in.

One of my best guy friends, John was applying. As a matter of fact, I probably spent more time at his house than mine. We loved hanging out together. I watched him enter the church and waited for him to walk back outside. Becky and I were the only ones who knew that he was gay. He stepped out the door with a huge smile across his face, and looked at us while he threw his arms up. He'd been given a green light. I knew that if he had no problems getting church approval then my meeting would be nothing more than a formality.

Then entered our expositor. Dylan could recite more scripture than anyone I had ever met. His brother was also like a walking Bible dictionary.

Next, entering the church was a young man whose girlfriend I knew was pregnant. He finally emerged and swiped imaginary sweat off his forehead and nodded. "Wow, I guess God will take anyone!" I thought.

Then it was my turn, last in line as usual. I sat down in the chair across from the pastor's palatial office desk and with a hint of a smile, I glanced at the certificate on the wall behind his leather office chair. "Ordained..." I was ready for the interview to begin! My pastor shifted forward in his seat, folded his hands on the desk, next to a large opened Bible and asked with a kind smile, "What did you want to see me about, Betty Lou?"

I said, if it weren't obvious enough, "I want to go to Bible School." What I *wanted* to say was, "Duuuuh, isn't it obvious? Can't you just see the call of God with the anointing pouring off of me?"

His chair squeaked out the only audible sound as he slowly leaned back in his chair. Raising his eyebrows, he let out an elongated "Ohhhhhh," before more silence, as if struggling to formulate something intelligent to say to me.

"He must be kidding with me," I thought. Clearly, I was going to school. I had already put in my admissions paperwork and I was a straight A student. I had begun a Bible study in my high school and I had written devotions for youth. I was a captain in our bus ministry, and I used my guitar to lead singing with the kids on the bus on the way to church. I studied end-times theology, New Testament history and Greek word translations. I read biographies of great ministers and missionaries like

Mother Teresa and Billy Graham. The only thing standing between me and my destiny was... Bible school. I was certainly going to be accepted.

"Betty Lou..." he looked up at the corner of the ceiling for a few seconds before his eyes met mine, "How can I say this? You... heard the call wrong."

How do you hear a call wrong when God speaks to you? Is that even possible?

"Women are not permitted to be pastors. It says so in the Bible," he continued.

What? His statement was a sucker punch that felt more like a doctor telling me to get my affairs in order because I only had a few months to live.

"I'm sorry," he spoke, with an apologetic smile.

I could feel my face turn red as I fought back tears. Humiliation. Disappointment. I tried to remain composed as I stood to my feet, although he couldn't have possibly ignored that my hands were shaking. As I exited the church, I felt a surge of rage; not with my pastor. Clearly his orders were coming straight from God. I was angry with my own Creator. How could He do this to me?

As I walked out the door, my pal John was waiting for me. He stayed around so that he could congratulate me. Clearly, that wasn't what I needed. I asked him, "Want to get some beer?"

"Sure."

So, we did. Not only did we manage to get a clerk to sell us the "Champagne of Beer," but John had a connection for getting some pot. We smoked and drank until it was time for our youth meeting. We got in my 1966 Dodge Coronet, and headed out.

Instead of our usual location, we were meeting in the large basement at my pastor's house. However, I missed a step on the way down, and tumbled down, the stairs. I don't know how I wasn't killed, but when I stopped abruptly at the bottom, I was looking up into the angry face of my youth pastor. He pointed back up the stairs and scowled, "Get out!"

So, we did. I jumped back in the car and, being stoned out of my mind, misjudged the distance of my car from the parked cars to the right. I heard an awful scraping sound. In fact, I can still hear it in my mind as though it were yesterday.

I yelled, "What did I hit?"

"Just drive, drive, drive!" John ordered, motioning me to hurry with a circular arm motion outside the window. So, I did.

After we arrived at his house, we surveyed the damage, I wondered what the heck did I hit to cause such damage?

Really? Why did it have to be a police car?

My high school prom was coming up and I'd learned about a guy in school named Steve, who just happened to be a professional dance instructor. The movie Saturday Night Fever was a huge hit, and the senior class had chosen a disco theme.

I wasn't going to wait to be asked out by someone who had to be paid to take me. No sir. I decided that I would take charge and be in control of the situation. I sought the boy out, and offered to pay his way to the prom if he'd teach me to dance. We could go as a date, shining in the spotlight, turning heads and own the dance floor. I reminisced about the little-girl Betty, who had stars in her eyes, dazzled by Monique at the homecoming. I never thought my day would ever come, but, indeed, it had.

I bought a disco dress, and that night we made a grand entrance, and proceeded to steal the dance floor. Steve flipped me over his shoulder and turned me upside down. For the first time in my life, I was a somebody. For one night, like Cinderella, I was a princess, a star, and I beamed with satisfaction. We had everyone's attention, and for some, we *were* the entertainment. In later years, my teacher would say "I will never forget that night. You looked and danced just like that girl from "Dirty Dancing!" You looked like professionals!"

After the prom, we parted ways. My friends went out with their dates for ice cream, or to make out. I sought out John and his current boyfriend, and trolled the streets in front of THE Ohio State University before eating a late breakfast. My friends lost their virginity or made lifetime memories. I went home to cry; sad, alone, empty and deflated after hours of glorious fun. Just like the fairy tale foretold, "the clock struck midnight," and all the magic of the night disappeared as if it had never happened. If only I had a purpose... but, I was a woman, cursed, without a destiny, or so I thought.

As graduation approached, all the girls in my high skill stenography class at Eastland Vocational were entering internship jobs. We were applying for jobs with large companies or governmental agencies.

My stenography speed afforded me my choice of positions with the state of Ohio. I chose a position in the actuarial division of worker's compensation. It seemed to be a position with power, and upward momentum for the success which I craved.

These were the late 70's. Feminism was on the rise, and I had big dreams. I dreamed of moving up, sitting in a big office in a skyscraper with a glass desk, commandeering an extraordinary life of my own. I was going to be a modern-day Mary Tyler Moore—I was going to make it, and make it big!

I was trained to be professional at all times. I set the tone and control the office environment. The truth was, I faked the image of being a confident administrative assistant, until I almost believed it, myself. It never felt a hundred percent real to me, as hard as I tried. Something was broken deep inside and I covered up my insecurity with a classy act of having it all together.

My friends began to settle into their lives right after graduation. Several of my friends from class married their high school sweethearts in the first few months after graduation. Nearly all were engaged. I had just broken ties with my long-term boyfriend, Steve, as he was going into the military, and I decided I wanted more from life.

I was later set up on a blind date with a military man. Going out with someone in the Air Force had some appeal. This was my first date outside of high school. Although the man was less than enjoyable to spend time with, I went with him to his dorm room on the Air Force Base. As we walked down the hall, we drew a lot of attention from the other men in the barracks.

My date began downing straight shots of whiskey. He drank.... and drank, and drank. I was about to call my father to come get me because there was no way I was getting into a car with a slobbering drunk idiot.

A handsome airman poked his head into the room and asked, "Hey, want a ride home?"

My hero! I jumped at the chance to be freed from an evening of boredom and slurred stories. Not only was this person not drunk, he was good looking to boot. His car was new, and his room was neat as a pin. He grabbed a jacket and off we went to my home.

My dad was long before in bed, trusting that I was safe with friends, as I had said. When I got out of the car, the young man said, "I'd like to see you again, if that's okay."

Wow...someone wanted to see me, and he wasn't a total loser! He was an airman, with a car, and by all appearances from the hall conversations, popular with his friends. And, he wanted to take me out...on a date!

There was hope!

Moving in was an easy decision. I had been saving for an apartment, and my new beau told me that bringing me home from the room caused some issues for him at the base, and he was forced to move out of the dorm. I will never know if that was true, but I doubt it.

At this point, my planning included nothing more than purchasing a coveted princess phone in blue. If there were any red flags, I probably brushed them off at the need to feel loved and wanted. Either way I was about to be blind-sided and hit hard—very hard.

Our first argument was an eye opener. I had never in my life been called the names he hurled at me. The hope I'd felt in my heart that somebody wanted me had disintegrated in a few moments of time. When the initial shock wore off and the dust settled, I was left feeling utterly degraded.

I told myself that people combining their lives together will have rough spots to work out from time. "Things will get better with time," I lied to myself. I believed my optimistic self-talk, and in the end, we got married. The wedding was small, consisting of a kegger at my father's home. At the wedding, before I walked to the front to exchange vows, my father looked at me and said, "you know, you don't have to do this." In my heart of hearts, I knew Dad was right, but there was no way I would run away in a wedding dress. I mean, what would people think? Even if I'd been given this parental advice in advance, was reasonably sure I had the power to make this work if I just tried hard enough.

Then came Christmas time. Especially during the holidays, I always had felt how much my dad so cherished me, growing up! I loved the tree which lit up my heart and soul as it did in the room. It was overflowing with gifts, and we continued with most of our traditions, which helped carry us through missing Mom and Michael through the holidays. It was the one thing I could count on, through the years that drove away the dark clouds of loss. Every year I looked forward to the tradition of adorning a pretty Christmas dress. I was never disappointed.

Under the tree at our apartment, however, Roger's side of the tree was full of the gifts from me. I carefully wrapped handmade and purchased gifts and everything that I thought would make him smile. Packages were all different colors and loaded with bows.

Under my side... nothing. When I asked him about where my gifts were, he muttered without even making eye contact, "I figured you could go to JC Penney's and get that spice rack you wanted."

More arguments erupted when he informed me that we would be spending Christmas with his parents, even though they only celebrated on Christmas Eve. I wanted to be with my dad and my brother. It was my first year away from home and I desperately wanted to feel some normal. I wanted to feel the happiness that always came with the season. All of that came crashing to pieces in a heated moment when he quickly reached the point of no return—and then it happened.

I will never forget that first slap across my face. It stung, and left a red mark, but it did more than that. It embedded in my soul the resounding message that this was my value. My needs clearly didn't matter. The things and people I loved were unimportant, because I was worthless. My only value was to put his never-ending needs and wants first. Being battered became a way of life to me, and I didn't passively roll over. I learned to fight back verbally.

When I found a photo of a nude woman stuffed in the drawer, I questioned him. This didn't seem to fluster him at all. In fact, he was pretty indignant.

"Oh. That's my girlfriend from Florida. Miss Nude Florida, to be exact."

Well then, that was the competition I was up against. She was confident, stunning and nude! How does a girl who doesn't fit in compete with that?

"How do you get to be Miss Nude Florida? Are there contests for that?"

"It's a dancing contest. The strip clubs run it."

Well then, that explains how he could buy a motorcycle while he lived in a condo on the beach. He managed to find a sugar mama to take care of him. I was never going to be able to keep up with that!

I worked for the State of Ohio, in the actuarial division with the largest starting salary than anyone in my class. My score on the civil service entrance exam was so high I had been offered my choice of five jobs. I had chosen the one with the best pay and benefits and future advancement.

Obviously, this wasn't going to be enough. My dad was proud of me, but the man I wanted with all my heart, to be with forever didn't seem to care. I began looking through want ads in the paper and came across an ad. Maybe this was the answer.

That ad is still in my memory book. It marks another turn in my downward spiral.

I had never ventured into this area of Columbus before. It was the opposite side of the city from my little farm town. The block building sat alone, but it didn't look so bad from the outside. It could have been any neighborhood bar. Even the name wasn't foreboding: Lookin' Kool.

Glass cases were adorned with photos of beautiful women with names like Charlise, Velvet, and Candice. "What pretty feminine names," I thought, not realizing that the names were no more real than the costumes they wore. I realized immediately that the phantom I was fighting in "Miss Nude Florida" was a formidable one. She was even more lovely than these ladies.

It never occurred to me that strip clubs were open during the day, or even on weekdays. I naively assumed that going to see dancers was something men once or twice in their lifetime. I figured they might go on a weekend for a bachelor party or when they hit 21. Go once and then mark it off some crazy bucket list of things to do, and be done with it. When I opened the door and music streamed out, I wasn't sure whether I should run, cry or what.

The man behind the counter asked, "Can I help you?"

It must have been obvious that I didn't belong in a place like this. I didn't fit. Again.

"I'm answering an ad for a waitress."

"Oh, you want to see Len. I'll get him."

He returned with a rotund man who fit every description of a mob boss I'd ever seen. "Hi, I'm Len." The obtuse man grunted. "Come on in."

He showed me to a café table, and I sat with my back to the stage. A gorgeous woman in a beautiful formal, low cut dress and very high heels danced behind me. I kept my eyes and mind focused on the reason for my visit. I reminded myself, "you are here to get a waitressing job or back-office position. Focus, Betty, focus."

"So, what can I help you with?"

"I'm here to apply for a waitressing position, or anything you have open in the back office. I'm excellent at short-hand, I'm proficient at 10-key, and I can type 90 wpm."

"Yeah, yeah, yeah, I don't need none of that. So, can I ask you something? You know that our waitresses are topless, right?"

I attempted to retain a professional and pleasant poker face, but my head was spinning. What? Why in the world would you serve hot food, topless? That seemed crazy to me. No, I most certainly didn't know their waitresses were topless! It definitely wasn't listed in the ad.

Len shrugged and with a glint of a smile he said, "I mean, if you are going to do that, why not just be a dancer?"

This entire conversation caught me off guard, "Oh, I couldn't, I mean..."

"Can you dance?"

My mind went back to prom night, whirling around, and hearing all the gasps and awes and even applause that emanated from the crowd. It was possibly the best night of my life and I was the star of my own show.

"Yyyy...yes." I stammered.

"Why not dance then? You'd make more money."

"How *much* more money?" I queried. I couldn't believe that I had even asked the question and I was sure it couldn't make that big of a difference.

Len took a drag off his cigarette and leaned across the table. "Substantially more." As if on cue, he leaned back and gave me some space, as if I needed some to breathe and think.

Then silence. The ball was in my court. He expected me to answer. But how? I was an administrative assistant. I shuffled papers and took shorthand. I loved to crochet. I really wasn't the type of exotic woman who sauntered about covered in nothing but feather boas and stilettos.

"Look," he said. "It's lunch. There are only a few customers. You could audition right now. No one will bother you. If you hate it, then we bring you on as a waitress. If you like the job, you become a new headliner. We'll spot you a few costumes, until you can build up a wardrobe." I found out that as a headliner, I would be featured with a poster picture promoting me as the newest star of the club.

He was calling my bluff. I didn't even have a pair of deuces in my hand. It was put up or shut up time. And I couldn't go back home as a mousey, boring secretary. If I did, it wouldn't be long until my husband found someone better. It was time to make a bold move.

"I'll do it." Showtime.

In those days, dancers were covered by entertainer contracts, hiring the girls as independent contractors. My first contract was for two months, but each contract thereafter was for longer and longer stretches of time. I'm often asked what happened to all my religious training at this point? Weren't my morals screaming out to me? In my young mind, I believed that if God could see me through that black ceiling, He'd strike me dead. But in reality, even then, He was protecting me.

The allure of "being a star" or "independent entertainer" fades when dancers are subject to huge fines imposed if they don't live up to their portion of the contract. For us, there was no sick leave as contracted entertainers, so we had to show up and work or suffer some pretty severe financial damages. In addition to lost wages, we had to also pay the club whatever amount they believed they were "out" when we were absent from the stage that night. This amount fluctuated by the day.

One of our girls came in within three hours of having an abortion. She stuffed tampons up into her body with the cords tucked up inside in hopes of finishing her shift.

(Dancers are not allowed time off due to monthly cycles.) She collapsed on the stage in the middle of a song and began to bleed profusely on the stage.

This was my introduction to abortion, and to the complete heartlessness of the owner of our club.

"Get her off there!" He screamed, while the bouncer picked her up, carried her off, pushed the dressing room door open and dropped her in a heap on the floor. One of the girls reached down to gently touch her cheek before hurrying off because her song was coming up. The entire situation was surreal.

By this point, it was too late to argue or try to back out. I had signed the contract. I had bills to pay and a husband to keep happy. He became pouty and angry if he didn't get what he wanted, when he wanted it. Buying him gifts and giving him cash kept his mood in check. He was becoming accustomed affording expensive things from my income. He bought himself fine suits, steak dinners with expensive drinks and his appetite for jewelry seemingly, could never be satisfied. He had a small collection of star sapphire jewelry and gold rings. He seemed happy, especially after having secured a job as a bouncer where I danced.

I became one of the headliners, and my own spouse was my personal body guard. Any guy who thought he was following me home was met by a surprise when a tough looking dude opened the passenger door for me and glared at them.

Although our club allowed no alcohol (due to state law) because we were fully nude, I seldom went to work when I wasn't high or drunk. Dealing with the customers and selling them on expensive drinks and tips was nauseating. Most of the men were hideous to me, and when they'd reach out to stroke my skin, I'd shudder. I was required to touch them and make them believe I was about to fulfill their darkest wild fantasies.

I will tell you, some of their fantasies were pretty dark. Much darker than a little farm town girl was ready for.

I noted immediately on the first outreach with Xpose Hope that one difference between my past experience and the current clubs was the number of tattoos. Every girl, it seemed, was cartooned in bright colors. Everything from hearts and flowers, to satanic designs emblazoned their flesh.

Girls who contracted with Lookin' Kool and other clubs I frequented were not permitted to be tatted. Club owners felt that the customers needed to be able to reflect their own fantasies onto the girl. Our bodies were a profit center and we were not to mark our billboards with anything that could hinder the profits of the club.

This wasn't a worry for me because I had a huge fear of needles. This fear probably saved my life when I was in the industry because I probably would have flirted with heavier drugs to escape.

One of my friends, however, really, really wanted a butterfly on her ankle. She wanted that butterfly so badly, that she was willing to pay whatever fines were entailed. She figured she might be able to cover it up with makeup, leggings over high heels, stacks of jewelry on her ankle and other fashionable techniques.

She came into the club the night after it was done, and showed me. That pretty much assured I would never get a tattoo. It was swollen and red and slathered in petroleum jelly. It didn't look "pretty" to me! It looked extremely painful. If this was 24 hours later, I couldn't imagine what it felt like while it was being applied!

"Oh, that's cute!" I lied, "how are you covering that tonight?"

Her mouth turned up into an impish grin. "I told Len I fell down going up my stairs and took a bunch of skin off. So, I can just use this big Band-Aid!"

Perfect!

Within weeks the smudgy artwork took on definition and was unmistakably, a butterfly. It was cute, and with the popularity of ankle bracelets with the guys, that we all started wearing some. Ankle boots hid the colorful little flying insect, as well.

A few weeks later, Charlise came into the club ill, and her skin had a weird yellow tone. She said she had been feeling really cruddy, and hoped it would be slow so Len would send her home. I told her that her skin was a funny color, and we worked together to even out her face and chest, but little could be done with the rest of her body.

The next day, Charlise did not show.

Len was ranting about, as he usually did when a girl or two were missing. I however, was thrilled when girls didn't show up. It meant more opportunity for stage times and the corresponding flow of cash falling at my feet. It also rescued me temporarily from having to make inane small talk with men, most of whom I despised. I had less time for lap dances. The best perk of all? It meant I was safe up on the runway—as Ohio law didn't allow for customers to touch us while we were performing.

On stage, I had total control. I could get men's attention with my gyrations and I could steal a glance and hold their gaze, away from their conversation with the woman who came with them. I'm not sure what kind of man brings a date to a strip club, but they did. I was able to get them to open their wallets, and offer me money and drinks to perform moves they'd like to see. I was risking nothing, except my nudity, because my safety was ensured by the strong-arm security guys that Len kept around. The run way was my playing field and men were toys to be played with, and financially, taken advantage of.

When I'm asked what ties strippers to the industry, people assume it's the money. The money is only part of it. Power— that's the real draw. Some women will continue to work the pole when they are well past the age of earning the top dollar of their more youthful years. They do it because of the control they have of themselves and the customers when they are performing.

The scuttlebutt in the dressing room was that Charlise had some really bad disease. Her liver was in trouble and she was in the hospital. Wow, I knew she was sick, but I had no idea it was that bad.

I drove to the hospital the second my lunch shift was over. There she laid; her blond hair streaming across the pillow, IV's trailing out of her arm, watching Let's Make a Deal on the television.

"What happened?"

"I passed out! My roommate called an ambulance." She unfolded the medical facts that added up to hepatitis C stemming from a dirty needle used by her tattoo artist.

Now, I was positive. I would never get a tattoo.

She convalesced in the hospital for nearly a week before I brought her home to my place. She was so weak that she needed a steady arm to slowly shuffle back and forth to the bathroom. As we were loading her in the car, she asked, "Can you help me get into my heels tonight?"

I was sure the illness had done something to her mind. "Are you crazy? You can't go to work tonight."

"I have to. Len sent some goons to the hospital today to let me know I had to be at work the first shift after I got out, or he'd break my legs."

"He's just kidding. You know how he rants and raves."

"No. He is dead serious. I'm scared." She held up a copy of her contract. "They left me this."

I'd never heard of anything so ridiculous. This wasn't Chicago or Las Vegas. We didn't have the mob and Len wasn't an Italian godfather. People didn't really strong-arm people like that in real life with threats to break their limbs. Hollywood movie stuff. Not real.

"I'll go in and talk to Len tonight. I'll make it right." I assured her.

Uh huh...

My car was a mess, which is not unusual for a girl in the exotic dancing industry. I stored half my wardrobe in there, including anything expensive which might tempt another girl to steal. I certainly didn't want to share things like make up or my break-away underwear which plenty of the girls would have no problem "borrowing." The backseat was covered in different colors of heels and fantasy costumes.

I dug through the mess and grabbed my suitcase with one hand, and my shoes in the other. I tugged the door open. What a difference from the first time I had wandered into the venue, thinking I was actually taking charge of my life and running it as I saw fit. I blew my last bit of smoke out in order to say hi to the guy behind the counter, and I headed to the back. Len was in the hall.

"Hey Len, Charlise got out of the hospital today."

"Good! We're low a girl tonight."

"Well, she isn't going to be here. She can barely walk. She's recouping at my house."

"Tell her to get her ass in here."

I shot him a look that said, "You're crazy."

"I'm not kidding, Pee Wee. You get her here. She knows the drill."

"Len, did you hear me? She can't stand up."

He bit the end of a cigar. "Okay, she can come in tomorrow."

"And if she doesn't?"

He raised his eyebrows and nodded at the high heels dangling out of my left hand. "Those are going to be hard to wear with two broken legs."

I was face to face with pure evil. If I could have peed down my legs right there, I would have. I was that scared. I felt stunned. For the first time since making my debut of working men to my advantage, I realized who the boss was, and it wasn't me. In my ignorance, I had threatened his income stream. The notion of "my control, my power" had been shot through with an arrow of dread and fear.

I worked my shift trying to act like a hot seductress, but the fact was I felt cold and clammy. I have no idea how I held myself together for the entire night shift. Thank God it was a Monday, which was slow. I performed behind my "tough chick" façade, but I experienced a meltdown every time Len walked into the main room. I felt a new level of nakedness... as if I everyone could see right through my soul and read my mind. My legs felt like rubber and convulsed while I thought my heart would beat out of my chest.

Gripped with fear, I worked the pole, putting on the best acting job I could muster, to at least pull money for my finale. I could tell that these men had somehow, in their own darkened souls had bought into my fake, forced flirting.

I went through the motions but I it seemed almost like an out-of-body experience. At the end of my night, I threw as much stuff as I could off the wardrobe rack into my suitcase. I didn't want to draw attention to myself, but I couldn't bring myself to leave all those expensive costumes behind. I knew that I wouldn't come back. I had made my decision. I told a few lies and I got myself out of that hell.

I didn't know what I would do, but I knew I had to run. I didn't know where—just somewhere. Away. I started sobbing uncontrollably the minute I pulled out of the parking lot. I drove the 71 to the 70 and headed back to our little apartment in Whitehall. When I got home, I was a bleary-eyed mess, shaking so bad, I fumbled to unlock the door.

Roger called his boss and the details of our situation ran quickly up the chain of command. That night the three of us moved into a temporary living quarter similar to a hotel. Within a week, we moved into a house on the military base where Len's hench squad couldn't follow or track me.

Although I was relieved to be out of eminent danger, the adrenalin rush which I'd enjoyed while getting ready to hit the stage had been replaced with me facing my own emptiness. It wasn't long before I felt like I was drowning in lackluster days of doing nothing exciting. I was bored out of my mind. Charlise lived in an adjoining room but we lived more like the three amigos, sharing takeout dinners sprawled on furniture watching movies on tv together.

One Friday night, Roger poured shots of whiskey, and slapped a deck of cards on the table. "How 'bout a nice game of poker?" We pulled up chairs and sat at the small kitchen table. He dealt the cards. "Let's make it more interesting," he said with a sly smile.

The night degraded. Even when I had danced, naked, on stage, in public, I did not allow the deepest part of who I am to be seen by the longing and gawking gazes of hundreds of men. Somehow, in my willingness to expose myself on a public stage I still guarded closely, a desire at least, to protect the intimate piece of my heart and soul which I had reserved only for my marriage. I walked out. I drove through the rain to a payphone booth, calling the only friend that I could reach on the base... Roger's boss.

When Charlise was sick, I visited her, stood up for her to my own demise, fed her and gave her a place in my home to escape threats of violence. And my reward? She had emerged, triumphant as my rival for my husband's affection. She stole from me, the one part of me that I held in honor.

I huddled into the booth yelling over the sound of the pouring rain, bombarded by one thought, "What am I going to do now?" I was out of a viable job in mainline society. My job at the state was long gone and I certainly couldn't go back to the club or any other club, as Len would certainly hear about that! I couldn't even safely leave the base, and I was worried that going home would bring danger to my dad or younger brother.

Although my marriage suffered a major blow after the Charlise incident, shaking my trust, I surmised it could all be boiled down to the "Betty factor." Betty gave and gave. She cared and cared. Why was I so driven to care for others who were indifferent toward me, showed me no love, and to all my efforts did nothing but take and take?

I was grateful Roger's boss called the temporary living quarters, and told Roger that he had to send Charlise on her way, and take care of his military dependent. I figured that the entire night was chalked up to drunken behavior, though I knew from that night on, that my greatest fear was true. I was unable to keep my husband's eyes, or anything else, only on me.

Again, I was the one who didn't fit. I could never measure up. I could never escape the idea that I didn't belong.

Though we did a short stint of trying to be civilians, when I found myself pregnant, it became apparent that we couldn't make ends meet on what Roger could make on the "outside." Tears ran down my cheek as we packed our few belongings into a moving van, and turned out of my father's driveway for a new life in Florida.

I was truly a small-town girl, and I had no idea how I would navigate life without my dad and family to run to when I was afraid. I could no longer pop over to a friend's house or go to see my mom's grave to cry out my worries. I was going to be...alone.

"How could you be hungry?" Dad's voice brought a mix of both relief and humiliation. "I thought he went back in the service in order to pay the bills and feed you and the baby."

"He did, Dad, but it's an expensive place to be stationed, and we are behind from the cost of the move and the time we were out."

Money was tight, military pay was low, and the area was a tourist mecca, so rents were very high. Thanks to being rear-ended in his newer vehicle, we were driving my first car; the 1966 Dodge, that I learned to drive in. It didn't always like to start.

Dad cleared his throat, "I can send you some more money. But this money is for you, to take care of yourself, do you understand?"

"Yes, Daddy, thank you. I love you."

He asked solid questions. But I had no real answers for him. It seemed to me that Roger's pay should have stretched further. The military had supposedly paid for our move, but if they gave us a check, I never saw it.

Several months passed and I needed income, but no one was going to hire someone who is six months pregnant.

I waited for the mail to come, and when it did, I pulled out the cash that dad had stuffed in the envelope and took off on foot to the only place to get food in walking distance—a Waffle House restaurant. I would order their largest breakfast, bring it home and break it into three meals. That would feed me for three days. To this day, a Waffle House sign is like a huge hug to me. The place literally saved my life.

When my husband had the time to take me to the grocery store, I bought basics to make fried eggs, grilled cheese and fried onions, which I craved.

I was thankful that my father had given my old crib to us, so I had one less thing to worry about. Its slats were wider than safety standards suggested, but it was that or nothing. I spent my days preparing Anne's room, making the things she would need that I could sew out of old sheets—crib sheets, bumper pads, etc. I didn't have a sewing machine at the time, so I hand stitched all if it. It didn't really matter, as I had nothing but time on my hands.

Roger was coming home from work later and later. How the military ran its daily operations at this base, I had no idea and it never occurred for me to question it. I was relieved that he was back in the military, and I could have medical care for my baby.

Our car had seen better days. It really needed a brake job, but I had no idea how to do that, nor was I in any condition to fix it. Besides, I never drove it as it was our only vehicle that Roger had to commute to and from the base. My transportation was my feet.

As time got nearer and nearer to the delivery date, I greatly anticipated the joys of becoming a new mother. I could hardly wait for the evening of March 2nd to attend our first Lamaze childbirth class. So many thoughts and questions had rolled around in my head, unanswered as the time for my baby's arrival loomed closer. As many times as I wanted motherly advice, I also longed to just hear mom's voice. If only I could talk with her, glean wisdom and share this excitement. Instead, I faced motherhood alone, with no friends in the area. I really needed, and looked forward to these birthing classes. I was completely in the dark; clueless about what to expect and I was worried that without instruction I'd do something wrong.

Back then, information had to be sought in books, of which, I had none. I had no knowledge of giving birth outside of tv shows—woman in a prairie dress presses her hand on her swollen belly and gasps, suddenly, and with no apparent warning, "It's time!" She is escorted into another room by a midwife who exclaims, "I'll get the water." The camera pans to man pacing in another room. What *were* they going to do with all that water? I was inept this giving birth thing. After all, I was the one who never measured up, right?

As I hurried about the house getting ready for the evening, I began to panic a bit because Roger should have been home hours ago. How could his boss work him late when we had an important class to attend? Then it happened. A cramp...or... was it? In the next few hours, the cramps got stronger, and they became evenly spaced together. Oh no...what was I going to do?

Just in case, I packed an overnight bag, and then struggled to pick it up. A terrified me waddled down the stairs, dragging the luggage with me. I called the office. No answer. I paced for a few minutes. I stood on the porch. I paced a bit more. Finally, when I feared that I wouldn't make it to the hospital, I called Roger's boss.

"He's not working.... He's probably at the NCO club."

I didn't have time to be upset. I just needed him home. I called the club and he headed for home. As soon as he came through the door, he realized that he needed to get me to the hospital immediately. He explained to me, after strapping me into the car that the car had no brakes. None. "Here's the plan. I'm going to coast, and turn tight circles once we get close to the hospital entrance. Stay put until it slows way down, nearly to a stop." He further explained, "You will have to jump out of the car while it's still rolling."

I was laughing so hard, I thought I'd have the baby in the car, beside myself, wondering how crazy it would be for a woman in labor to enter a hospital with a broken leg sustained while jumping from a moving car. We later laughed a lot at this story, and it became family lore. This was a diversion that saved me from a lot of fear from the situation since I was totally unprepared to have a baby.

The nurse weighed me and hooked me up to IV's and asked how far I was in my childbirth classes. I answered, "Ummm, my first one is going on right now." I broke down crying. The nurse rolled her eyes and let out an audible sigh. Both of us knew that this was going to be a long night. It was. I labored through the night and into the morning— twelve hours in all. I was too young to know to say "No" to Demerol, which didn't have an effect on my pain level. It did, however fog my mind enough so I couldn't figure out how to breathe the way the nurse was trying to explain it to me. I finally just quit trying and screamed through my contractions.

I had no idea that there was such a thing called an episiotomy until the moment it was being done. Imagine my shock! In the end, I gave birth to a 5-pound 14 ounce, absolutely perfect baby girl. I named her Anne, nicknamed after a missionary saint who I greatly admired. I spent three days in the hospital, cuddling her more than the nurses said I should. She gripped my pinky with her tiny fingers and I assured her, "I will always have your back."

When the nurses came and pulled her from my arms her for their medical routines, I considered what to do with a husband who was staying away from home and spending his time looking at dancers at an NCO club. Well, if you can't beat them, join them. I was never one to back down from a fight, and I decided to fight fire with fire—within four weeks of her birth, I was dancing at the same club my husband had frequented, and partying with the customers. At least there, I fit in.

Needless to say, the marriage did not get better as time went on. Anne had turned three and I was pregnant again. By this time, we had been transferred to Nevada.

I picked up a job on base, working with a civilian who oversaw the temporary living quarters for visiting airmen and distinguished guests. It was something like a hotel job and I enjoyed making money, which helped out with our living expenses. But mostly, it got me out of the house.

Roger and I didn't mix. We were like water and oil when we were together that turned more like gasoline on fire when we didn't agree and things escalated. I wouldn't say the marital turmoil was all his fault, but I fought back answering his physical violence with a verbal onslaught to hold my ground. We fought over trivial things at the drop of a hat. fighting became more intense and arguments became louder, and for a time I ignored threats I should have heeded.

I would have thought more of these arguments, but this was the only marriage I had known. I married so young and I had no real role model with my own parents because the family life was centered around a dying wife and mother in a home already crippled with grief. Marriage, as I understood it, was for life. You made a bed then you were to lie in it. I also realized that I could be mouthy, and therefore, I'd assume that perhaps I had pushed him too far sometimes, making him lash back at me. He had never touched one of the children that I knew of, so the blame I assumed, sat squarely on me.

After Cheryle was born, we especially enjoyed our weekends, as this was the only downtime we both had. We slept in most Saturdays. As a breastfeeding mom, I was tired a lot, and on one particular morning, I was blissfully dreaming. I woke up to the sounds of a scuffle. I'm not sure what our three-year-old had done to raise his ire, but her father yelled obscenities at the tot and punched her back with his fist.

"Get out!" I screamed as I ran to my daughter's aid. He retreated, and my daughter was gasping for air and bawling, inconsolably. She pushed me away when I tried to hold her close. I lifted up her shirt and saw a massive bruise on her back that seemed to grow, as I stared in disbelief.

I ran outside and beat on my neighbor's door. When she opened the door, I told her that my daughter was injured, and asked if she could she please watch the baby. She agreed, and I handed her Cheryle, who was also scream-ing at this point. I ran back to the house, picked up Anne, and the neighbor's husband gave us a ride to the base.

The medic was a friend of the family. I told him the situ-ation he began to examine my daughter and did some x-rays. My heart sank at his prognosis. In his calm, doctorly voice, he said "she might be losing her kidney." We would need to go down to the hospital in Las Vegas. He ex-plained that before I could go, I had to talk with the security police who were already standing by to get my statement. They asked for details on what had happened.

My heart was pounding, and for a few seconds I couldn't seem to pull myself together to find the words. I was ter-rified to tell them, but I was more terrified not to tell them. I didn't want to go to jail for failing to protect her, and especially now, I could see clearly that I was her only protector. Friends drove us to the hospital in Vegas, where the doctors called the airbase and Child Protective Services.

Physically, Anne healed just fine. However, she was bro-ken on the inside, and was never the same. While her dad had never really doted on her with much affection, now he had almost no contact with her. Eventually, he wanted nothing to do with either of us. He also stopped giving us any money. In answer to my pleas for assistance, the mil-itary's solution was to allow Roger to come back home.

How was it that I was asking for financial help and their answer was to send him back to live with us? We were not safe, and we were not going to be safe as long as we were under the same roof together. I was going to have to find a way out without raising suspicion or making him angry.

Sure enough, within a couple of months, the two of us blew into an argument. By now, we had been transferred down to the base in the city. The final argument left me with no choice but to get out before he could act on his threats. He warned in a sadistic tone, "I'll make it look like you did it to yourself." No one would have known. My father wouldn't have had a clue about the real story. My kids would have been left with a man who was flagrant in his distain toward them, and indifferent to the welfare for their lives.

I'd met a group of friends on a local chat room-social networks that came prior to the Internet. One man in our group named Layne, told me that if I could find an apartment, he'd help me move and get us situated. I also took him up on his gracious offer to shuttle me to and from job interviews.

I realized that I needed a car, but I couldn't afford the payments from the one that was financed from the marriage. I began to look for something I could afford, which meant, "very used with lots of miles and not too pretty." One of Layne's friends was selling an older model car that ran well and he had arranged, that if I wanted it, I could buy it on very small payments.

Layne took a genuine interest in my girls. They warmed up to his warm kindness and gentle demeanor. They opened their lives to him and talked about their top news of the day— drawings, toys, adventures, ups and downs. To see them light up when he showed up melted my heart. What was not to fall in love with? Here was a man who truly loved my children and didn't see them as a burden. He told them stories, and took them out in the grassy area by the house to play. He shared his passion for books with the girls, and they joined his excitement for reading, and treks to the library.

Layne enjoyed English, but he didn't believe in himself to go beyond a few college classes to get a degree even though he was smarter than most of his professors, and could have taught their classes. He made displays working part time at Sears; not a paragon of success and upward mobility. But, at this point in my life, kindness trumped material wealth and social status. I couldn't put a price on kindness and feeling safe with matters of my heart. This man was a lot like my father who knew how to make me feel safe, loved and valued like a priceless treasure. This was a wise choice.

We married in the spring of 1989 in a private ceremony officiated by a commissioner of marriages. I'd originally planned a nice wedding, but it grew exponentially once his family began to add all of their invitations.

Layne was uncomfortable with large groups of people. He explained to me that it was more about our commitment to one another, and not what anyone else thought. That belief carried throughout our lives together. Layne was a man of commitment and getting things done. One evening, we were watching television and folding clothes on the couch. He asked if I really wanted to marry him.

"Of course," I replied. Did the man think I was doing dress fittings and arranging silk flowers for fun?

"Then it is going to have to be right now." I knew that he was serious. "Do I have time to put on my dress?"

"No."

So, I grabbed my bouquet from the table and we ran to the commissioner of marriages/sewer department to say, "I do." The pictures of sewer pipes were not really the décor I had envisioned, but sharing that moment, alone, with Layne was a gift, and is etched into my heart forever.

Hellbound was playing at the dollar theater. Popcorn was a buck. This was my honeymoon. I cried all the way through the movie, thinking, "Is this a picture of what my new married life is going to look like? Does he think is now bound for hell?"

Layne squeezed my hand and smiled thinking that I was simply overwhelmed with joy at being his new wife.

After every honeymoon, there is a marriage, and this one was blissfully, 'til death do us part.

I probably didn't get off on the right foot with my new mother-in-law. To her credit, at the time, she didn't know that she was my mother-in-law. She didn't like me, and I didn't care. It began as a heated argument about how the guest list was getting out of hand. Layne and I had decided not to tell anyone and have the ceremony for the sake of our families. We could celebrate twice each year that way.

"You will never marry my son!" she yelled. Not to be out-done in a yelling match, especially when I held four aces, I was able to leave her speechless with my loud return volley, matching her ferocity, "Too late, b---ch! We have already tied the knot!"

Shortly after our wedding, news came that Layne's fraternal grandmother had passed away. This forced his family to connect with us again, as his father called to instruct us to attend the memorial. We drove to Utah for the funeral which also became my introduction the Mormon church.

I had learned a lot about Mormons when I was in my teens, studying Dr. Walter Martin's "Kingdom of the

Cults" course study of the church of the Latter-Day Saints. We read his book, Kingdom of the God Makers, listened to all of his teaching tapes and learned about their doctrine, "as man is, God became and as God is, man can become." It's amazing how quickly the knowledge we amass dissipates given a little time and a lot of "life happens" in between.

I watched as the families began to pour in. Entire families stuffed into one car, coming from the East coast to honor this grandmother. The funeral was different, too. No pastor. Instead, family members stood, one after another, to sing the praises of this wonderful woman. They lauded her as a woman of God, a wonderful wife, and a meticulous homemaker. Then, they sang a song about family being forever. What a lovely sentiment for an orphaned young woman.

At this point, I was so far from God that I wouldn't have recognized his Word. The "scriptures" that were quoted seemed to be from the Bible. They had the perfunctory "thee's" and "thou's." The cadence struck a similar sound of the King James Bible.

I knew that the girls needed to be back in a church of some type, and since the family I had married into was Mormon, maybe this was a good place to land. If all Mormons were this family focused, I thought I'd feel comfortable, and I was ready to finally be welcomed to a church where I fit in. Maybe this was the place where I would spiritually plant my roots, and have a sense of belonging at last. When we arrived back in Las Vegas, I called the church and asked for the missionaries to come. They gave me lessons and I was later re-baptized into the Church of Jesus Christ Latter Day Saints.

We quickly assimilated, and before long we were preparing to be "sealed" in the temple. The process included "sealing" my current children to Layne for time and eternity, and it would also ensure any children born to us after the sealing would be ours forever. That is— unless one of us didn't make it to the Celestial Kingdom. Attaining the Celestial Kingdom is not an easy thing to do. One must perform the duties of their callings, and many Mormons have several, as well as duties to family, job and country to a level of near perfection. Quickly, all of our time was soaked up by church activities.

On Sunday, our day of rest, women spent the entire day in dresses while men stayed in their church clothes, as well. In reality, we went home and stripped down to our "garments," and threw on robes over the top. These were special undergarments sold by the LDS church, with special markings in the belief that they had special power to endow the wearer with physical and spiritual safety. Sundays were not meant for work, so dinner was usually something stewed in a crockpot the night before. I couldn't write that day, but I could work on family genealogy or do visiting teaching. That entailed visiting sisters in the church who were assigned to me, and a cohort to visit and provide a spiritual message. Layne could go with his partner to do home teaching; except he had the authority as a man to give a message to an entire family.

Monday was family home evening. That meant that every Monday, the door was closed on extracurricular activities including school events in order that the family "shut out the world" to spend time together. Tuesdays was youth and other days were more activities. Needless to say, our social lives became wrapped up in our church. There wasn't a lot of time to think about the discrepancies I saw between the Book of Mormon and the Bible. When I did begin to notice them, they bothered me.

It didn't take many years, before I could no longer ignore serious flaws in the church. The first thing that couldn't escape my attention was that most Mormons placed little importance on the Bible, and they rarely quoted it. They didn't really know a thing about these scriptures which I had cherished growing up. The Mormons embraced the Doctrine and Covenants. They quoted the words of Joseph Smith and recited the history of the "Nephites."

I also realized that although the lessons for the women's meeting, called Relief Society repeated every four years, the ladies didn't seem to incorporate them into their lives.

The lessons— fifty in all encompassed the year, minus the 2-week hiatus of hearing from the annual "president/prophet" of the LDS church. This was usually read verbatim which to me was a mind-numbing, extreme exercise in religious monotony.

They noticed that I was teaching the lessons differently than all the others. Well, I didn't just read them. I was still being led, unbeknownst to me, by the Holy Spirit who had never left me. "It's like God is sitting in the room with us when you teach," ladies would say. I was glad that they were getting something from the teachings. Still, I was confounded as to why almost none of the women seemed motivated to follow the current prophet's guidance to study and apply the scriptures at home more often.

Then Layne was called to the primary grades, which is the Mormon equivalent to Sunday School. The bishop in our ward told him that he would be required to prepare a lesson and activities each week. He refused. I did it for him, spending hours cutting out crafts while writing out the lesson to make it easy for him. You see, not fulfilling callings would preclude one from entering the Celestial Kingdom. I did all of this, *driven*, that I would not fall short of entering on some minor infraction of submissiveness. I was not permitted to be in the room with him as I was a teaching Relief Society at the same time.

At the time, Layne was working 12–16-hour days, coming home to do home teaching and fulfill other needs of the church. Perhaps a widow needed work done on her home, someone needed help with getting transportation, hospital visitation... the needs seemed endless. It was wearing on the entire family. More wearing on me. I became pregnant with child number five.

By now we had four children with my two girls and the two Layne and I had together. Anne, our eldest, now 15, became the president of her primary class.

We struggled at first, as any low-income couple would. The younger children were too small to grasp the desperation of our financial situation, and we tried to make the best of every hardship. Our electricity had been shut off for non-payment on several occasions. What our home lacked in economic decadence and indulgences was made up with a secure love and kindness. Our children giggled with delight every time they got to eat by candlelight when our electricity was shut off.

I took to typewriter and paper and began writing every waking minute, in hopes of resurrecting my freelance career. At the same time, Layne was taking every side job he could as a manager in a cabinet shop.

Quickly, our diligence began to pay off. Layne rose to the top of his company and was promoted to vice president.

He left the cabinet shop, becoming a mill manager at a wood supplier, and he did so well, they promoted him to vice president. My endeavors were also taking off, providing writing to multiple outlets, from fashion trade journals to travel and business magazines. Two magazines placed me as a fashion editor and my work was jet-setting me to awesome places. I spoke with designers in New York City and dined at Les Halles, and Windows on the World, located on the top floors of the World Trade Center. I attended fashion conventions, and was lavished with samples from advertisers.

The monetary stress from our lives had been alleviated. I used to dread going to the mailbox, knowing it could contain a letter with a red stripe, threatening the shut off of water, electricity or gas. The tables had finally turned. Instead, I was rewarded with checks. Sometimes, there were piles of checks on the dresser waiting for deposit.

I went from using pliers to pull up the seat in my E-150 van to driving new vehicles with electric seats. Our cramped living quarters, with three boys in one small 10 x 10 room and 2 teen girls in the other, was replaced with a 3600 square foot home with a pool in gated community.

If we wanted something, we bought it. We were gadget lovers, and we both had laptops, desk top computers, and a Lorex security camera system to watch our home. The garage was full of recreational toys including dirt bikes, camping gear and our touring motorcycle.

We didn't pitch tents, set up camp, get eaten by mosquitoes or poke around firepits to cook meals in campsites much anymore. Instead, we'd spend two to three weeks renting a furnished cabin on the Oregon coast beach to relax and unwind. We ate at restaurants in Vegas that didn't have menus—if you needed to ask the price, you couldn't afford it. I wore designer clothes and I hired a maid service to keep my home sparkling clean.

Then one day, as I was scurrying to get all the boys ready for school, the phone rang. Layne asked, "Are you watching the news?"

I was a newsaholic, and Layne knew this. So, if he wanted info, I'd be the one he'd call to get the latest news. But that morning, I got up later than usual because I'd burned the midnight oil to meet a deadline the night before.

"No, why?"

"Turn it on. I was just told we are under attack."

My first thought was, "clearly, someone has watched too much 'War of the Worlds'," as the tv flicked on. I froze and my jaw dropped as I watched a passenger plane fly into one of the World Trade Center buildings.

That moment is seared into my mind. It changed my life. My heart sank. I was horrified, watching as the buildings I'd just visited, collapse into a giant heap of mangled steel and dust. I reflected back when I had stopped to admire the massive, opulent revolving doors at the Trade Center before entering. Now, they were gone. Dust.

Gone were the people who had served me. I recall the restaurant was preparing for a large dinner party that evening. Gone were the thousands who had worked at investments, banking and administration. All their dreams, their hopes for the future...gone.

This shook my world. I kept my kids home from school and I quietly reflected and pondered about my life. I began to withdraw.

Success is a wonderful thing, but it can also be an awkward bedfellow. Success means you don't always sleep with your husband, because sometimes, one of you is on the road. Sometimes, you get so busy getting your career going, that you no longer have time to share about it with anyone. Success can turn you into an island.

When we were young, I was home, and he worked two jobs. I would sit up to hear about his day. As we both began to thrive professionally, we were often too busy to slow down long enough to download our lives to one another.

I had always hated Las Vegas, and several times we'd talked of moving. In fact, twice we put money on properties in Oregon, but each time, Layne had been offered another dream opportunity that put off our decision to retire in Oregon. Time and again we put off the move for the sake of Layne's work.

Now, I found myself in a place I really despised, with my family far away, and my husband had become a person I barely knew anymore. He moved in industry. I moved in fashion and a world of advertisements and interviews. I wanted to go back to what I loved more than anything. I wanted to go home.

I knew that with the current economy there was no hope for a move, and I didn't want to be like those I watched die on 911. I wanted no regrets when I went. I wanted to make a life of memories just in case I didn't have much time to make them. My mom didn't ...I assumed I would also die young.

Within a few months, I asked Layne for a divorce. I pushed him away and when he begged me to stick it out. I was adamant—I wanted to move back to my friends and family in Ohio. No amount of persuading was going to change my mind.

So, he changed tactics. "Would you give me just three months?"

Three months...we had been married for more than a decade, so what was three months? Fair enough.

Little did I know that he was seeking help. He had been watching the foreman of a vendor company named Robert. He visited the jobsite to assist with the stair units that Robert's company installed. He watched him handle disappointments at work and in his personal life. The thing he saw in Robert was a supernatural peace that cloaked him at all times.

So, he reached out, telling Robert of our maritial issues. "How do you have such a peace all the time?" Layne asked. "I can't sleep, I can't eat."

"My boss is a carpenter." Explained Robert. Layne was confused. What did the background of his boss have to do with Robert's demeanor? But Robert went further, and invited Layne to Promise Keepers. They were coming to Las Vegas for the first time and Robert purchased the tickets.

Layne's preference was to turn down the invitation, but the tickets were expensive, and Robert had already purchased one for him and our eldest son. There was no way, without offending Robert, to say no. So, they went and the first night, Layne had a life-changing encounter with Christ.

As a man who had always felt disconnected from his father, Joe White's message that night, resonated with Layne. Joe reminded the men that someone else understood rejection and faced temptation. Someone else had been forsaken, and still that Person gave all for them. During his sermon, White built, with his own hands, a wooden cross. He hammered the nails in, and he spoke to his Father—as Jesus would have. The message penetrated deep and touched Layne's heart. Both he and our son accepted Christ that night.

But no one told me.

I found out by experience.

For two months I laid in bed at 4 am, when my husband pulled himself out of bed each morning. He would head straight into the walk-in closet to curl up with a pillow on the floor. The dark silence of the morning was broken with his sobs as he'd pour out his heart with tears, crying to God. I heard him pray for our sons, for their protection and their souls. He prayed for our two adult daughters, and every day, I heard him plead with God.... for me. He prayed that even if I left, I'd be protected. He prayed that my heart would heal. He prayed that God would help him become man who I deserved.

He was transforming day by day as he slowly emerged as that man who might be found worthy of honor. The changes weren't forced, faked or out of some religious obligation to "do better." No longer was he late or absent from our son's baseball games. He left work to arrive early, excited and engaged. For the first time he found time and eagerly looked forward to help our son with school work. The kids' confidence and grades began to soar in academics, and they looked forward to doing all the hands-on science experiments with their dad when he came home from work.

I watched the man I married rise to a new level as he exuded a tangible peace and joy to those around him. He spoke differently. He behaved differently. He came home on time, but instead of plopping into his easy chair and clicking on the tv, he powered through undone chores around the home. Finally, one day, I ventured to ask, "Layne, what is up with you?" He took my hand, and walked me into the kitchen and we sat down to the table. He fixed his gaze into my eyes. "You know when we went to Promise Keepers? I met Him for the first time... really met Jesus. And He became real to me for the first time in my life. I decided I would follow Him, and never go back to the way things were... to who I was before I met Him."

He continued to pour out his heart to all that had happened at the stadium that night. By now tears flowed down his cheeks. He begged, "Will you please give me another chance to be the man you deserve? To be husband that God called me to be?" My eyes welled up with tears, and felt myself falling in love again with the man I'd met and had said, "I do" to many years before. I had more than what I'd known and expected from a husband. For the first time in my life, I experienced sacrificial love. I was so thankful to have a partner again who was available to me, and not just to his work. That night, I returned to my Savior, and life began anew.

It took a bit of searching to find a church. I wouldn't say we church shopped, but we certainly had quite a time finding what I was accustomed to, since I was raised in the 1970's "Jesus freak" revival movement. We settled into a small United Methodist church where the pastor bluntly told me he questioned his own faith. When I pushed for a youth program, I consequently was appointed the youth pastor.

Needing to find a better fit, we landed in a large non-denominational congregation. Due to my son's need for something different, we entered the homeschooling life. I wasn't sure how teaching lessons and administering tests while holding down a full-time writing career would pan out. I figured that if I failed, at least my son would fare no worse than he currently was in public school— slipping through the cracks in a system that didn't seem to care about him.

Every day was a barrage of juggling time and priorities, and all the myriad of things I was trying to be all at once; a mother, wife, homemaker, head of a homeschool cooperative, teacher, youth pastor and... a bread winner as a fashion editor. The travel required by my job which had once been an exciting adventure filled with great escapes to fun places and interesting people now felt like lonely treks that ate up time. The need to be super-woman made my entire life absolutely harried as there just wasn't enough of me to go around. In the blur of feeling roped into more than I could chew, I spent free moments contemplating what I wanted for me.

What was it? The spark in my heart. My original, heartfelt... call. Yes! A call— to be an ordained minister with degree in theology. I felt like something or Someone had breathed into my heart at that moment. The smoldering embers of my first love, purpose and desires began to radiate inside. Something had to give.

We couldn't stop homeschooling, and it was imperative that our children have social lives. How could I fit it all in? We talked about it and prayed. We came to one logical conclusion, and Layne went to his boss, "My wife needs to quit work to go back to school. I'm going to need a raise."

The next week, I informed all my writing clients that I was done, and I entered Moody Bible School. Unfortunately, before I could begin classes, the journey of life took another odd turn.

In March of 2009, Layne and I embarked on a trip up to Oregon. With our touring motorcycle in tow, we spent a few days looking at homes, as well as kicking back and walking down the beach enjoying the mesmerizing sound of crashing waves. Being Oregon and spring, it rained and rained some more. People would look at us with pity and tell us they were sorry our vacation had been dampened by the misery of "liquid sunshine," they called it. We were actually loving the weather.

Rain in Oregon is not like rain in Nevada. We get only two storms a year in Nevada usually...sometimes, only one. And it comes down all at once. Massive flooding ensues the deluge which drowns out all other sounds. It stings the flesh and pounds at the car like a hammer.

In Oregon, the rain showers were misty and light. Showers came between passing bands of clouds, letting up long enough for us to just stand in quiet awe, admiring God's creation in constant motion. God, the Artist who painted the seascapes, did it all for our pleasure, and we soaked in the knowledge that He is so, so good. Oregon is a place of unimaginable beauty. Mountains seemingly pour themselves into the sea, and everything west of the Cascade Mountains, as far as you can see is a paradise of lush trees and foliage. The vast country farms harvest berries, nuts, hops, grapes, flowers, and endless varieties of crops like a sprawling Garden of Eden.

I interrupt this picture of Utopian bliss. Picture me sitting on a park bench, clenching the slats on the seat, in tears when it was time to go back "home" to the God-awful moonscape called Nevada. Layne gently, and then not so gently had to pry me off the bench, like a star fish clinging to a rock. I loved Oregon. It felt like home.

In contrast, Nevada resembles a giant kitty litter box—a beach without the ocean, topped off with oppressive, unbearable summer heat. Trees are tiny, stunted growths with spindly leaves. We wanted so much to live in Oregon, to pull the kids out of the Las Vegas mire. Each time we stepped out to buy a home, Layne's employer lured him with a large raise and a promise of a bonus large enough to retire on. We vacillated between doing what seemed right, financially for the future of our family, and just wanting to get out of Dodge. At some point many people come to a fork in the road. One sign pointing one way, shouts, "standard of living!" while the other sign's words point another direction and whispers, "quality of life." The question is, which path can you take where you are looking forward and not back all the time?

We met Layne's best friends, Sam and Gail Riggs in the coastal town of Florence for a dinner. While we were dining, Layne set his fork down and glanced at me. Food got stuck in his esophagus and when the issue had resolved, Sam said, "You had better get that checked out."

I didn't think anything of it because Layne was only 46 years old. His entire family had lived into their 80's and 90's, healthy and there was no cancer in his family to speak of. Somehow, Sam knew something wasn't right.

Soon after returning home, Layne scheduled a doctor's appointment. The doctor told him that he was pretty sure it was nothing major. But, just to be safe, he ordered an endoscopy.

I wasn't that concerned, because a few months before, Layne had called me from work and asked me, "Are you at a place where you can get the guys working on something and leave?"

"Sure. What's up?"

Layne assured me with a light tone in his voice, "I don't want to upset you but I'm at the hospital."

It happened that he had been experiencing chest pains so severe that he had curled up on the floor in his office.

Typical Layne, he decided he probably needed to be seen, so he drove himself to the hospital.

My tone, not so cheerful, I half demanded, "What if you had killed someone or yourself?"

"Well, everyone is busy today and I didn't want to bother anyone.

That was Layne, always concerned for others. He had such a servant's heart that even as the vice president of a company, he didn't want to disturb anyone to drive him to the hospital which was only ten minutes away.

The staff ran multiple tests, including an angiogram. The doctor actually said to us, "I don't know what you are going to die of, but it won't be caused by heart problems. You have the heart of a 20-year-old."

There is no prep for an endoscopy, so I just planned to take the day off from homeschooling so I could drive Layne home after the procedure. That morning, after the staff checked him in, he sat in the wheel chair and a nurse took him back. My stomach was growling a bit, so I decided to wander down to the hospital cafeteria for a bite to eat.

Eggs. Sausage. Iced tea. I pushed the food around on my plate and took a few bites. The hunger I'd felt earlier was replaced with a pit in my stomach. Something wasn't right. I finally decided to abandon the food and bring the iced tea with me back to the waiting room. I had just walked in and was met by the nurse. "There you are.... The doctor has been looking for you."

The ice tea seemed somehow sacrilegious, and my excursion to get food, callous, as I stood there speechless. I had nonchalantly left the waiting room to go eat. Why did I leave? What if there was a complication?

The doctor met me in the hall and said, "I don't know how to tell that man in there. I told him that he was certainly fine and that this type of cancer is the cancer of old men.

But I couldn't even get the scope past the tumor because it is so large."

I muttered, "So, there is cancer in his throat?"

"In his esophagus. But there are things that can be done."

Oh, I was thankful for that. We were certainly up for any fight.

"They can do radiation to shrink it so he won't die choking to death. I'm so sorry."

"So, you are telling me he has cancer and is going to die? Take it out! This is the 21st century. We will fight this!"

"It's not curable. He will die. He has 3-6 months."

At that moment, another voice was whispering to me as well. It said, "You will be a widow." I knew that voice was God. My next thought was, "Thank God for Promise Keepers."

We went into the recovery area to give him the news. He said that he knew something was wrong when he watched us walking toward him. "You are not alone," Someone assured him in a gentle voice. He felt a hand on his shoulder from behind, even though his bed was in a corner, and his back was to the wall.

On the way home, I called the kids for a family meeting. We stopped and we cried, and we said, "we are going to fight this." Doctors are sometimes wrong and we repeated, "we are going to win."

And that is what we told our children that day. Dad has cancer. But not to worry. We are going to win.

I began to call cancer hospitals the next day. I found six of the best hospitals for esophageal cancer in the country and selected one of them to call. None of them were near our home, so this next phase in the fight required air travel.

Half of a day was spent flying, renting a car and driving to the hospital, so meeting a valet at the entrance was a nice touch to the first leg in our journey. Then we were taken in to register, and be assigned our doctors. Although he had the procedure in Vegas, we could never get the results because they'd scheduled to have them ready in about four weeks, which was several weeks too late. Consequently, Layne was set up for another PET exam.

I waited for him to finish the exam, and we were told to go to lunch; our appointment would be in about an hour. In Vegas we felt like we were on a wild goose chase, running from doctor to doctor with no real information being provided, and no consistent plan of care. The radiation doctor would say one thing, the oncologist would tell us another, and we never did meet a surgeon. This coordinated care was a godsend.

When we arrived, we were greeted with a warm smile from Layne's oncologist.

"I have your results. Would you like to see them?"

See them? How remarkable and unexpected! Not one doctor or medical facility in Vegas was able to produce the results of Layne's tests, much less communicate them to us! He then showed us a color monitor with the scans brightly illuminated. The tumor lit up, unmistakably clear.

"You are at stage 4A because your tumor is so big. It's here, at the GI junction," the doctor continued, "The tumor is into the wall of the esophagus, and possibly protruding through."

This was a huge blow. We had hoped for stage 2 or at worst, 3. At the time, the survival rate at stage 4 was less than 2 percent.

"We are going to begin chemo, and with your age and your otherwise good health, I think this could be a good prognosis."

We both took a deep breath of air and felt hopeful for the first time in weeks. Layne smiled at me, as if to say, "I told you so. I'm going to beat this thing."

The protocol was chemotherapy with monitored imaging, as we progressed to see how the tumor would respond. Then we would begin chemo/radiation. Following that, we would need to do surgery. I knew from research that those that got the surgery had the best chance at survival.

We went home prepared to fight.

Chemo was always administered at the hospital, and the cost of flying was expensive. Although we were slated to go every 2 weeks, sometimes we would be bumped on the schedule. Occasionally, an opening would come up to do an additional test so we would have to book flights on less than 24 hours' notice. Those flights were expensive.

In addition, the hospital preferred we stay at an adjoining hotel. The five-star accommodations with all amenities was not a cheap venture but it also came with the ability for a nurse to come draw blood before bedtime, and provided all the necessary items for cancer care in the room. Sharps containers hung on the wall, and hooks were available to hang a chemo bag, etc. We dined a few times at a lovely attached restaurant—anything that made our stay less like scheduled hospital appointments.

Time. How much time we had left together was the thing we both pondered in our hearts but neither of us spoke of. We were redeeming time for dates that we may not get later.

Layne researched, and discovered that drinking Esiac tea, and juiced wheatgrass daily was helpful. A bit later, our good friend Gail found articles about benefits of black raspberry powder for people being treated for esophageal tumors, so he added that to his liquid beverage diet. I attribute the benefit of these remedies on the fact that the cancer's spread seemed contained, and he never had to be sent home due to having a low blood count. Whether it was being proactive to include these remedies, a placebo effect or just the fact it kept Layne's head in the game, I'm not sure, and I didn't care. Everything seemed to be working.

We searched for books on how to navigate cancer as Christian believers. We found nothing of consequence from a spiritual point of view. However, we found several books from survivors that taught us to take control of our medical destiny, and be proactive in doing our own research. We joined the Esophageal Cancer group on Facebook which site provided support, information, and lifetime friends.

It was in this time when we found out who are true friends were, and many weren't as true as we'd believed when Layne's treatment began. These "friends" would pretend that they didn't see us in the grocery store, and Layne would track them down. He wanted them to feel uncomfortable for "ghosting" him, because he was not yet dead. I understood. Layne made cancer real. After all, it could be could be their family tomorrow, and he was a walking example.

When believers asked what sin he'd committed to stop his healing, I began to ask "Where is Paul of Tarsus?" Clearly, there was never a greater man of faith than Paul, and yet his time to leave this earth clearly came. We learned more than ever that condemnation and judgement is an invisible sin to those who smugly wear it as a badge of spiritual honor. Still, it is nothing more than somebody with a stick in their eye trying to remove a speck from another's.

The only side effects of chemotherapy were minimal during the first round; slight nausea which was easily combatted with Zofran. However, with each treatment, he became more averse to cold. He described the sensation of drinking ice water like swallowing razor blades, and he often wore gloves even in the warm weather. He also had an extreme changing taste pallet; sometimes I made a run to the cafeteria to bring him something that sounded good to eat, but by the time I got back to the room with his food, he could no longer stomach eating it.

When the time came to begin chemo-radiation, the doctors explained that the radiation would be administered daily. This meant we would have to move into the hotel next to the hospital for three months. Our eldest son, then 17, took on role as the man of the house, taking care of his 14-year-old brother, and overseeing our business under the watchful eyes of his grandparents. Our 11-year-old journeyed with us.

Chemo was difficult enough, but nothing compared to the nightmare of chemo radiation. The chemo caused Layne to drag through each day feeling exhausted, compounded with the steroids that made him extremely edgy and volatile. The treatments turned him from being a peace-making introvert into a man I could barely recognize.

His anger was severe enough where he descended into a deep rage over very small things. For instance, he only wanted to eat Panda Express every day. One day while we were driving, our son asked if we could have a kolache (meat baked inside of a pastry roll) instead. Layne blew into a rage, and hit the steering wheel, screaming at him. In that moment, I truly feared that he might step on the gas pedal and drive us into a pole. Once the steroids left his system, he remorsefully cried and cried over his uncontrollable outbursts. He was embarrassed and he hated thinking that his child might never forget these things.

Part of the cancer center's core belief system is in empowering patients and their caregivers. For those who live out of state, they teach the caregiver to do things, like how to care for the pic lines embedded in a patient for chemotherapy administration, and how to remove the bag if they wear a chemo bag home.

They require care takers to learn how to properly care for the lines. This includes all the sanitary practices, as infections are an easy way to lose a cancer patient whose immune systems are unable to fight them. Caregivers must learn how to work with a sterile field. Before being permitted to go home with the chemo bag, the caregiver must demonstrate to nurses that they are competent to carry out this procedure on the actual patient. No pressure. However, if it is done wrong the patient may be infected... and die.

My "exam" was scheduled for the same day as our visit to meet Layne's thoracic surgeon who had been randomly assigned to our case. He had done many of these surgeries, as have all the surgeons at the facility. Our plans were struck yet, with another blow. We didn't get the news we had expected.

While our oncologist and radiologist were telling us that the tumors were shrinking rapidly, and that he was going to be healed, this surgeon looked right at us and told us, "Go home and spend time with your family. I'm not going to do this surgery." We were blind-sided with this doctor's words which went against the grain from what all the others had said to us.

I was aghast. How dare he, after we had come so far, dash our hopes?

And more so, how dare God do this to us!

We arrived at the lab where my exam was to take place. My heart was racing and I was feeling dizzy like I could have passed out. My hands trembled and I could hardly see through the tears which blurred my vision. How I was supposed to pass the test, I had no idea, all the while I was screaming at God on the inside.

"Why did You do this to us? He has been a good father, and a good man! He has expedited hundreds of men to make changes in their lives by helping them get to Promise Keepers. With his open-door policy at work, he carved out time for any employee who needed a safe place to talk about issues at work or home, or ask for advice. He has fed the homeless, and helped struggling families make ends meet." I continued to silently vent, and demanded, "If You are real, God, after all we have given up for You— You had better show up right now!"

I dared not voice these curses out in the open so Layne might overhear, but I had just crashed headlong, full speed, into another wall. Over and over, I had given up things in my life for God. And now? My reward? Was this it? God saying, "You haven't given enough, Betty Lou. I am going to take your husband."

I stood Motionless in a stupor; time and space slipped into temporarily suspension. Lost in thought, my heart sunk deep with a bitter concoction of disbelief, anger and grief. Strangely, beyond my control, I was transported back to another time and place—to that little girl, Betty Lou, who rested her head on her mother's cold body, listening in vain for a heartbeat. "Mom is dead," echoed from decades gone by. I'd completely forgotten that I was standing in the waiting room when my eye caught a glimpse of a weak elderly man who ambled slowly toward us. I'm not sure what he must have seen when he looked into my eyes. "My name is Norris. I hope that I'm not intruding, but I'm a Baptist pastor, and God sent me over to care for you."

In that moment, I could have been knocked down with a feather. Anyone who knows me can attest that I am never at a loss for words, however I couldn't even get my name out to introduce myself. Norris explained that it's okay to not take the doctors' grim prognosis to heart. The doctors had told him years before that he had only months to live, following his diagnosis of liver cancer. He said they marveled at every appointment, with no medical explanation as to why or how he was still alive. "Only God knows the future," he spoke out with a quiet exhale.

He then reflected, and added, "He won't take me home until the assignments He has for me are done."

With no doubt, on that day, I knew that God heard me loud and clear. I had never realized that God can look amazingly, like a pastor with liver cancer.

Much later in our journey, Layne stood by his side when he'd finished his race and stepped into his eternal home. I believe that perhaps his final mission was to be the voice of God to speak to me that day.

In October, we managed to arrange for another surgeon to operate on Layne. He not only got a new surgeon, but his case was assigned to the head of thoracic surgery.

The surgery was long. It entailed taking out his entire esophagus and pulling the stomach up to create a new esophagus. His actual stomach would shrink to about the size of a tablespoon.

Prior to surgery, we watched a little girl in the waiting area who was taken back immediately after they wheeled Layne back. I heard the frantic eardrum-piercing screams as they attempted to settle her down in the bed.

After they had Layne's lines all in, but no medication yet running through, they called me back to be with him for a short visit. As we sat there, he asked, "You know that little girl who came in from the waiting area?" I nodded my head.

Layne had a soft spot in his heart for all children. He would shed tears when a little one was taken back for radiation. He'd say over and over that at least he understood why he was being tortured with medications and radiation, but those little ones were not old enough to know what was happening or why. They just hurt, and it was bitterly difficult to watch and hear.

Gazing at the ceiling, Layne muttered, "She was screaming and crying." Wiping a tear from his eye, he turned his focus toward me, "I asked Jesus to send angels to protect and calm her. A few seconds later, two figures moved across in front of my room. Very beautiful, all in white." His voice became a whisper, "When I looked down, Betty... I couldn't even see their feet. they were not walking. They were floating across the floor."

According to Layne, when the figures got to the end of the row next to the girl's bed, she suddenly stopped crying.

"I know they were angels." He said, with a hint of a smile.

"Yes," I agreed. Most assuredly, he'd cried out for God to send angels for this child, and moments later he watched in wonder as God brought them immediately to tend to this child.

I also realized if he was seeing them, it was because I wouldn't have him much longer.

Layne had some struggles with Fentanyl when he came out of surgery. I am certain the doctors and nurses get used to patients lashing out with a barrage of verbal abuse that is nothing more than a side effect of the medications. Layne snarked to his female physician, "Hey, you! Stupid nurse...you know, you might have gone further if you'd actually *finished* medical school?" I was mortified...this was not the Layne I knew. He was never crass or condescending. Thankfully, the doctor understood it was a reaction to the medication, and made a quick change.

For three straight days he refused to be left alone, so I was thankful when a homeschooling friend who also happened to be a nurse, came to sit with him so I could do laundry and eat. I was grateful for the national homeschooling group who upheld me during our battle with cancer.

Once that battle was over, and he was moved to another pain killer, my sweet husband blossomed back to his wonderful self. He'd become so much like the foreman, Robert, whose very presence changed the atmosphere with his invisible God. He was continually walking rounds and lingering close to the nurses' station, cloaked with peace, and spoke encouragement to everyone he met. Finally, he'd passed his swallow test, and was released within a week.

It wasn't more than two weeks until he wanted to take another esophageal patient out for a steak dinner. I thought he was crazy since most esophageal cancer patients rely on feeding tubes for months following surgery before venturing to eat. But he was done. He wanted to eat, and he finished half of his steak while explaining to the gentleman and his wife why they should consider going ahead with surgery.

Right before Christmas, we got a call from Layne's radiologist. She wanted to tell us that he was a miracle, and from what she could see, he was cured. We celebrated that year with extra gusto. Health truly is one of the best gifts from God.

In March, we flew back for Layne's three-month checkup. We dropped in to see some friends we'd met during radiation treatment at the hospital. We were ready to celebrate together, with these friends. However, they informed us that the husband's cancer had returned and he had only one or two months to live. I was devastated. He had been a cardiac surgeon who was sure that proton therapy was going to irradicate the cancer for good. It was this man who had told me about this particular cancer treatment center, and had given us courage to fight. He was a stage four survivor until that week. My heart broke for him and for his wife. But it also broke for me.

It was a cruel reminder; that nagging feeling that no matter what we did, and how valiantly we tried, we wouldn't circumvent the inevitable. As much as I tried, I couldn't

ignore the words I'd heard, "You are going to be a widow."
Alone. I shuddered, and I broke down sobbing. Layne put
his arms around me and pulled me close, and told me that
it was okay; our stories were not going to be the same.

The next day at the appointment, the nurse, who'd always
lit up when she saw us, because we brought her gifts from
Vegas, was distant. She silently kept her eyes on the chart,
the scale, the blood pressure cuff and quietly jotted nota-
tions in the chart. She was all business, and made no eye
contact with Layne.

The appointment was gut wrenching. The doctor told us
that he was confounded. He had never seen anything like
this before in his medical career. He crossed his arms and
shook his head, "It's literally *everywhere*. I have never
seen a cancer come back this aggressively or quickly." His
words went right through me. I couldn't even grasp what
he was saying. What does he mean, "everywhere?" What
are our next steps?

We had no time to even process the doctor's words because we had to gather up our bags and belongings, and
rush to the airport or we were going to miss our flight
home. Before going out the door, I stopped by the bathroom and slammed a stall door behind me. I collapsed on
the floor, and I threw up over and over and over again. I
sobbed into my hands and I begged God to let this day
not be real. But it was.

We started a new chemotherapy that included a pill version of chemo. It wasn't working well. We asked to have his tumor sampled, and the doctors created a targeted chemotherapy to attack it. If fighting for Layne's life wasn't hard enough, our insurance refused to pay for the treatment. They also informed us that they were not going to pay for the proton radiation that he had already received. We weren't too concerned because the staff at the proton unit had assured us, they often had to fight the insurance company through several appeals, but eventually— they had always paid. The woman behind the desk told me that the facility would let us pay as little as a dollar a month. If Layne should not make it, they promised that the hospital never went after widows.

When lesions showed up in his liver, I asked for radiation beads to be inserted, which worked well for targeting tumors in places like the liver, and proved to be less damaging to surrounding tissue. Unfortunately, by now he was considered a lost cause. I wrote pleas to several surgeons around the country, and found one who was willing to generously donate the surgery fees and the beads, in light of our predicament. He was in Denver, Colorado.

This doctor asked if he could pray over us. Yes, yes, and yes. On this never-ending emotional roller coaster, I took his generosity and prayers as a sign from God. Feeling a flicker of hope rising was nothing short of thrilling.

We went back to the hotel that night, with specific instructions that I was not to share a bed with my husband for 48 hours. We were told that the intense radiation could cause problems for me. However, Layne was exhausted, and he was terrified. I laid next to him and I sang hymns to him until he dozed off asleep.

Within a few months, he began to have problems swallowing again. A tumor had grown around the outside of his new esophagus. I asked if we could simply remove it, but the answer was "no, there would be no more surgery."

The pain of trying to swallow food became so severe that he would slide the handle of a spoon or fork down his throat to help him throw up. Every time he did this, I knew he was shortening his time here. I also knew he was in agony.

He dropped weight so quickly that I barely recognized him. My once robust husband looked more like a skeleton. The inevitable day came when he could no longer swallow food. He was starving to death and his kidneys began to shut down.

Still, he was certain if he could get them to radiate the tumor or to do some chemo to shrink it, he could survive. He'd come so far and had gone through so much, and he was still willing to fight. Layne was hospitalized in an attempt to get his kidneys to function again. His oxygen level continued to drop, so they suggested that he be intubated to give his lungs "a break." Of course, after being intubated during this "temporarrest" from breathing on his own, he would no longer be able to talk. The staff failed to tell me.... that he would never come off the ventilator once intubated.

Because of this, our last exchanges of farewells were left unsaid. I had called for the kids to quickly come to the hospital, but the intubation was done before they could arrive. He never got to say goodbye. He never got to tell them that the fight had been for them. His last words to me were, "I love you," before he closed his eyes, sedated, and was hooked up to a machine to breathe for him.

We were at his bedside for three weeks. Our 16-year-old son was not permitted to spend the night in the hospital so he would sleep in the hospital stairwell. I watched as parts of Layne died; turning purple, then black, and I fought for him as he had signed a living will to take all life-sustaining measures. He was prolife to the end. And

I was going to honor his requests. He deserved that I honor his fight. And, I did.

On Dec 20, 2010, I kissed my soul mate and gave him to the Savior he loved. He was only 48 years old. As my dear friend Connie eloquently stated, "it's not fair."

No one can understand what it is to grieve the loss of a spouse until they have done it. Many people who had never lost a spouse were the first to explain to me that I was doing it all wrong.

What I wanted to do was crawl into the casket with him.

Layne was the glue that held our family together—the softer touch. Perhaps the product of growing up with only one other sibling, and the fact that he didn't have death and loss forced upon him as a small child. He always said that I loved the children more than him, but I knew that they saw my strict ways as oppressive. I had carried a toughness from my childhood. I'd learned first-hand that life was hard and filled with terrible things. Perhaps, unconsciously, I was trying to prepare them to endure these unseen hardships they'd inevitably face in life. Being abandoned by family members via death, followed by mourning and funerals is a dark cruelty at any age...one that was most definitely more hush-hush in the 60s. Those hard things help shape me into who I was.

In time, friends encouraged me to begin seeing Christian men, and to begin a social circle that was not all couples.

I didn't fit in around single, divorced women, and it was awkward to be around couples. No matter where I went, I was the "odd man out." I found myself "different" again. Then again, I've never made friends easily. The word, "widow...." I despised being defined by my past and present with a word shrouded with death, grief and loss and being alone.

Perhaps what I walked away from in this terrible storm, was a clearer picture of who I was. Although we'd lost battle, I learned that I was a fighter, and not a quitter. Surrender is not easy for a fighter, so again, I struggled to rein in that part of me that didn't want to let go. I reminded myself that *my* story was still being written by the hands that held me in His. His pen; not mine. My story at present, was soaked with tears of disappointment.

The many people who promised Layne they would stand with me, to comfort, assist, and counsel had disappeared within a few weeks after the funeral. With my family far away in Ohio, I found myself completely alone. The business was not doing well, either. The recession was beginning to hit housing prices, builders, and any construction type of business like ours. I tried to pick up the pieces and put one foot in front of the other as I had done in much of my life for the sake of my kids.

I was stuck. Layne's "last commission" for us to move to Oregon and have them covered with medical insurance as soon as I could dogged me. His cancer treatments consumed all of our time and energy, and it wasn't until after the funeral, that I realized how isolated my family had become while in survival mode. I'd learned by then to quit saying, "what else could possibly go wrong?" But the saga continued in the real-life soap opera, "It's Betty's life."

The "clencher," they say, whoever "they" are.... the icing on the cake? The 80-mph curve ball? Here it was. The "no worries.... pay what you can," cancer facility had proceeded to sue me for hundreds of thousands of dollars. I had no hope of protecting the life insurance from them because our estate attorney had erroneously told us to put money from the insurance in our family trust. That opened it up for grabs, for instance... in a lawsuit. Without the insurance money, how would I make it?

I coincidentally met Mark, a divorced man with two girls. He was sympathetic to my situation and I felt some admiration for him as a single father, raising his children on his own. "I know that you will never love anyone like you do Layne, but I'd be happy to step in and help." Through his work, he could provide insurance and income for me and my kids, while I would homeschool all the children and be a stay-at-home mother to them. Looking back, it appeared like a cut and dried business contract, but at the time, it seemed like this would be best decision bringing stability to the kids—It was, in my heart of hearts, my greatest priority to take care of them. The kicker was that Mark was in the process of being transferred... to Oregon. My kids would be insured, and could continue through college.

After sleepless nights and trying to plot and plan, an instant answer to my dilemma was dropped at my feet. Surely, I figured, this was providence. Layne's dying wish was coming to pass.

Mark provided the answer. With a civil marriage we could buy a house with the money and put it solely in his name. Thankfully, when the time came to purchase the house, I heeded a strong internal urge that my oldest daughter should also be placed on the deed.

Once we'd moved, and the children settled in, the "relationship" began to deteriorate. Mark began to attack his children physically and mentally. I found out later that his behavior was even more sinister and calculated under the surface. While I was busy educating his children, and getting them situated into homeschool co-op programs, he was squirreling away the rest of the insurance money into his personal account. I later discovered that I had not been his first victim that he'd targeted.

Then one day, things escalated into physical violence, and I became the target of his rage. He grabbed at the car keys in my hand, and broke my finger in the process. At the hospital, I covered for him and claimed I had fallen. The nurse didn't buy my story so she separated us. As I continued to insist that I broke my finger in a fall, I told myself that the next day I'd be talking to an attorney.

When we went home, he begged for forgiveness and told me he never meant to hurt me in any way.

Later that night after I'd fallen asleep, my 16-year-old son on woke up to the terror of Mark holding a butcher knife to his throat, warning him that if I tried to get back what he'd taken, he'd kill us all. I didn't find out until later what he'd done and my son was too terrified to say anything at the time.

The next day when I arrived home from errands to find my "husband" and his children gone, I immediately checked the bank accounts. He disappeared— along with hundreds of thousands of dollars. The account was drained to almost nothing. I got in the car and drove directly to the bank, showed my ID, and explained the situation. They quickly facilitated in opening a personal account for me, and moved over the remainder of the money.

I went home to ponder what to do now.

Suddenly, and without warning my savings and income was gone. I had dragged my children to a state where I knew no one. Our health insurance was going away, for sure. And my house, my only real asset, was partially in his name. How was I going to keep my commitment to Layne to care for, insure and educate the children? What a huge mistake I had made in my grief, and wanting a quick fix for my dilemma.

I moved ideas around like chess pieces in my mind with options, contemplating consequences, and imagined possible outcomes. The bottom line? How to fix the big picture financially to take care of my kids.

Welcoming a virtual stranger into my life who turned out to be an opportunistic "serial thief," who preyed on women with bank accounts, gnawed at a pit in my stomach. The anger that burned, also fueled a hopelessness. Most of the time I couldn't get anything right, no matter how hard I tried. So many facets of my life had spun out of control for so long, I reached for an old friend named "control." A dark thought loomed in my mind. It grew into a logical conclusion the more I toyed with it, and looked at it from all directions. I saw no other options.

A million dollars won't solve all of life's problems, but it can ease the pain of loss, and be the cure for financial difficulty. Split among my kids, a 7-figured amount could fast track their way to an education, a home, and I could invest in their future. My decision was made. I planned to carry it out in a way that would least affect them.

Pills. Simple. Painless, with no fuss, but mostly, no muss. I pocketed bottles of psych meds that had been left behind by my abuser and his children. I walked out the back door, threw my leg over my bike seat and peddled to a park close to home. I sat under a tree, and quickly downed all the medication. Soon after, somebody found me, and the emptied bottles, and called 911. When the ambulance arrived, I begged the paramedics to please let me die. After all, I had learned first-hand that a good mother, gives everything, even her own life for her children.

My attempt was nearly successful, but God intervened. He provided a kind nurse who reminded me who I was. She gave me guidance to seek out the domestic abuse center in my town, and I enrolled in counseling. They helped me not only with what had just happened, but also with the all the abuse I'd endured in my life.

My sons proved to be loving lifelines of hope. The youngest was not allowed to visit, but waved at me from the hospital parking garage. My eldest brought cards, and played each night with me. Barely an adult, he stepped into his father's shoes and protected me.

I fought for my home in court, and was able to protect it, though it depleted my bank account to almost nothing. God reminded me that He held me in His hands and heart. My value came from Him. He was Papa, and was his daughter. I also came to the place where I finally understood that my value to my children could not be replaced with any amount of money.

I had hope. I was not alone. I was reminded again of *who* was holding the pen and writing my story, even when I had botched chapter after chapter.

Starbucks closed early. I call this "divine intervention." Without this apparent act of God, Tony Campbell would never have wandered in a Jamba Juice to meet me. It began as small talk over a raspberry smoothy. We chatted as the employees wiped counters, pushed chairs around, and mopped the floor. We watched them lock up the store as we dug into one another's lives. He was easy to talk to and I caught myself laughing a few times. I couldn't remember the last time I'd laughed. He did more than talk about church or being Christian. He explained how he had been involved in men's ministries in two states. Hmmm.

A few days later, a citywide Christian event called "Seven" (Seven Churches in Seven Days) was launching a week-of-prayer event. I had attended, and received counseling through one of the churches while another was my home church. I wondered.... I pulled out my cell phone and began typing, "Hi, Tony. Betty here. Would you like to go with me to the 7-prayer thing going on at church?"

Moments later the phone dinged. I looked down, "Sure."

We spent time in smaller groups praying, followed by corporate worship before returning to prayer circles. A sweet woman in our group was struggling to maneuver her wheelchair around the chairs to join us each time. After our last prayer time, the pastor announced that he would like everyone to come up to the altar for our last prayer session. I turned to Tony. He was gone.

Wow. "That didn't last long," I thought. I shrugged my shoulders as I pushed aside a tinge of disappointment. When I got up to the altar, there was Tony. He had pushed the disabled woman in her chair, through the crowds, to the front of the altar.

Chivalry was not dead. He had no idea how much that action touched me. Taking a risk, to leave the lady who invited you to accompany her to church, to quietly disappear to assist another woman. I drifted into a place I hadn't been in a long time. I felt.... genuine happiness. It was so "Layne-esque."

A few days later, Tony came to take me out on my birthday. He brought a small bouquet of flowers, and treated me with dinner and dessert. I had a good time, just connecting and sharing. When we arrived home, he kissed me softly on the cheek, and wished me a happy birthday. Nothing more.

Our dates were not the usual dates. One night, we would be watching his children roller skating, then next time, we'd walk along a pond with a coffee in our hands.

He once invited me to go somewhere very special to me, and he took me... to a Celebrate Recovery meeting. That was quite the eye opener, but I learned that CR is for more than addictions. He attended to deal with the anger of his divorce. Perhaps our oddest date though, Tony being ever the romantic, was a memorial service he didn't want to attend alone. After the service, we walked along the shore of the Columbia River, and he told me perhaps it was time to see a pastor for counseling.

"Counseling?" I looked at him with confusion.

"Isn't that normal when you are combining two families?" he responded.

So Tony, in his ever forward-thinking manner, had skipped telling me he loved me, and gone right into an awkward pronouncement that we would marry. I left that date very confused.

Our time together became more frequent, and one day he thought that we should do a family activity so I could really get to know his children. The fall air was brisk, and it was a perfect time to do something outdoors. We'd go bicycling—something I loved to do! I purchased a bicycle for one of his kids, and we set out on our excursion on a tree-lined trail that was closed to traffic. We were short one helmet, but this was a safe path with little risk so I handed mine over to one of the kids.

Oregon is so recreational, and naturally, many Oregonians take to peddling on two wheels. The state is dotted with bicycle trails and the streets have bike lanes incorporated into them. I was clueless that not everyone loved to cycle, and we were about halfway to our destination when Tony's kids began to wear out. Being a mother, I recognized the comments as veiled complaints, so I made an impromptu executive decision to take a detour. I veered off the trail and crossed the two-lane highway to reach our destination and reward—Dairy Queen. The road has a bike lane, and I didn't see any issue with traveling on it for less than a block to get there.

"I'll just cross the road first and signal when it is clear for them to come over," I thought. I made my way into the left-hand turn lane. Two cars were coming in the opposite lane, so I back peddled, waiting on those cars to go past.

I wish I could tell you that I remember what happened next. What *did* I look like flying into the air, or how did it feel like when the truck hit my left leg and hip? I've asked Tony to describe it, but he just can't bring himself to do it.

I do know that my body ended up in the street and my bike was wedged between an Isuzu pickup truck and a wrought iron fence in front of the Dairy Queen. I know that Tony threw his bicycle down and ran to protect me, screaming, "No God, I just found her."

Several times, I woke up, shivering with cold and shock. A bystander put a blanket over me, and another onlooker took Tony's kids into the restaurant.

I looked up, dazed, "What happened?"

Tony gently answered, "you've been hit by a car."

"Okay," I mumbled. Every few minutes I would repeat, "What happened?"

Tony didn't let anyone move me until the paramedics arrived. They assessed that my back was probably broken, among other things. The effects of the impact, and possible internal bleeding began setting in and I was beginning to swell. "You probably want to say goodbye," the paramedic suggested to Tony as they loaded me into the ambulance, "I don't know if she's going to make it to the hospital."

Tony was left to deal with the police, and to call my children. How do you tell the children who have lost their father, that their mom has been hit by a truck in a bicycling accident, and she might not live? It's not a job that I would want.

I remained unconscious throughout the ambulance ride to the hospital, unaware of the staff who'd scurried about taking orders from the ER doctor. I slept through the X rays, CAT scan, and didn't wake up until they were stitching my head wound. I couldn't remember any phone numbers, but I did know where my son worked, and I knew that I had been with Tony and his kids.

My injuries were extensive; my left hip was crushed, my right leg, and sacrum were broken, my shoulder sustained internal injuries, and my head had a huge gash. The surgeon explained that we were three days out from being able to perform surgery due to the length of time needed for my operation. I asked if I would walk again, and he replied, "I hope so, but I can't promise anything."

That was a punch in the gut. I had always been the doer... the woman who was in control, who handled things, cared for her family, changed lives, worked hard and ran nonstop. Who would I be if I never walked again? I soaked my pillow with tears as I pondered how pathetically useless my life would be if I couldn't walk. Why do I get my hopes up only to get crushed over and over? So, was this now my lot in life? I looked into space at nothing in particular and asked... "God, I took care of Layne to his death, but who is going to take care of me? Why have You left me alone... again?"

Finally, the day had arrived for the operation. I couldn't even bring myself to imagine all the months of rehab. How would I do that when I am widowed and alone? Then, something crazy happened. Only a few hours before I was wheeled into the operating room, Tony looked at me and asked, "Will you marry me?"

What was he thinking? This crazy man had practically moved into my hospital room to ensure that nursing assistants and nurses didn't try to turn me. Tony argued on my behalf when I refused to take the narcotics which made me sick. Now he wanted to marry a person who might be crippled the rest of her life. In my mind, that was insanity gone to seed. Sacrificial love, in fact, can look crazy. Facing storms for another, and committing to the long haul; that was my definition of being trustworthy.

A piece of metal was placed in my left hip with bone fragments attached, in the hopes they would grow together as one. The break in my right hip was a clean break, so the decision was made to let that heal on its own. Screws were placed in my back and left hip. Six months. That's about how long they said I'd likely be in rehab before I could return home.

After a week of laying on my back looking at the ceiling, I was ready for a new change of scenery. Sitting up in bed was about a two-hour ordeal fraught with pain and effort, but I was determined to push and adjust myself upward an inch at a time. I took pity on the nurses who were given the tasks of attempting to move me into a wheelchair. The continual, intense pain was beyond my experience of giving birth to five children.

I longed to be home, and being released from the rehabilitation center became the driving force that pushed me to look beyond all of my discomforts to get me there. I envisioned resting in the quiet of my surroundings with food that I wanted to eat. I asked for a list of what I needed to accomplish in order before I could go back home.

The list was extensive considering my condition: Walk the length of the therapy equipment. Stand on my own. Put on my socks. Brush my own teeth. Be able to shower.

Showers were particularly painful because I had to be transferred from the wheelchair to a shower stool. My hips hurt so badly, I would scream and cry. But Tony would patiently transfer me, ever so slowly. It felt like I was training for a marathon as I determined to conquer everything on the list.

Thanksgiving came, and I wasn't home to make dinner. This was the first time since I had turned 18-years-old that I couldn't enjoy the hustle and bustle of creating a Thanksgiving feast for my family. My children brought a Nesco cooker to my room, and assisted me in stuffing a turkey. I instructed them how to make mashed potatoes, yams, succotash, green bean casserole and dressing. And that year, we gave thanks in my room at a rehabilitation center. Surrounded by so much love and care, we gave thanks for life, no matter what the future held. My efforts for several months, along with prayers for a quick recovery had come to fruition. I was returning home, four months early.

On December 22, I walked down the stairs in my home, a feat I was not sure I'd ever attain, on the arm of my eldest son who gave me away in marriage. A bride. An over-comer, dressed in white, proof again that God had this thing... called my life.

Since our marriage, and settling in a church, Tony and I had looked for a ministry to assist. All my Christian walk, even as a teen, I'd been busy about my Father's business. The time since Layne's death was the longest stretch I had experienced, without being active in some kind of ministry. From youth ministry, to homeschooling cooperatives, to Promise Keepers, we had always volunteered. Now, I felt like I had nowhere to fit in.

Then, one Sunday our pastor announced an interesting new ministry; something very different. He called it "Living Water," and in short, it was a bar ministry. We were the first to sign up. A small group of us of would go to bars on a Friday night and talk to people. We brought coffee, bottled water and snack bars. We offered to chat, pray, and did a lot of listening. Sometimes, we gave rides to those who needed a way to get home safely.

The bars saw it as a service to their customers, so surprisingly, most accommodated us as long as we stayed outside. We got to know bouncers, and we had some amount of success in getting a few of our Friday evening black sheep flock to church on Sundays.

One evening, as we were pulling out of the parking lot, I noticed a woman in distress in a wheel chair on sidewalk on the other side of the street in front of a used car lot. She was sobbing and crying out.

"Pull the car over," I said to Tony, who was driving. "Let me see if I can help."

I approached her, and asked if there was anything I could do to help. I offered a water.

"I told him I'd bring him here, as long as he didn't touch anyone. Why couldn't he just do that?" the woman related, sobbing. "Why would he do this to me? He's in there getting a lap dance."

Oh. Her husband wasn't in the bar. He was in the strip club behind the car lot.

I talked to her, and tried to calm her. She had made enough of a commotion that someone had called the police. The police and a friend of hers had arrived and we ended up arranging a ride home for her with the officers. In the process we also told them about our ministry.

When I got back in the car, the pastor asked, "Would you ever go in a place like that?"

I shot Tony a look—as if to say "What have you done?"

"I didn't say anything," he defended himself.

"I'd go wherever Jesus sends me," I stated, leaving the discussion there.

The next month, as we prepared to go out for the evening, the pastor asked "What do you think of dropping by the strip club tonight? No pressure, but if you feel so led..."

And so, we did. Men and women, carrying coffee, tea, and miniature chocolate bars, approached the outdoor smoking areas. The women were barely dressed and they spend most of their time chatting with men on our team. I had in my pocket, a copy of my testimony in letter format, along with a gift certificate for a massage.

I looked for a moment to give out the envelope, but the ladies were very busy trying to get the guys on our team to come into the club. It was clear from this first venture out that we were going to have to leave the men behind if we had any hope to reach these women.

The next month, we took two women with us. One was a female pastor, and the other was a young woman. I didn't realize it until we were getting out of the car that she was only 17. Her faith was strong, but as I watched, I realized quickly that the women were attempting to groom her. I recognized the chit chat moving from basic piercings to the many other piercings that many strippers have, in highly erotic areas. The dancer who was chatting with the teenager leaned in and subtly began to gain trust by touching her leg once in a while. She was working to draw this child in.

I was so happy when our time at the club was over, and the girls went back in to get on stage. I knew that the idea was right, but we were doing something wrong.

The next month was equally disturbing. When we arrived, oddly, the smoking area was completely empty. We sat down to wait. The female pastor closed her eyes, and began praying loudly. Now, prayer is a wonderful thing, but there is a time, a place, and a method for different types of prayer. And some prayers, I believe, shouldn't even be prayed out loud.

"Lord, shut this business down! Take the money out of these girl's pockets..."

Oh my.

Well now, I could only imagine what I might have done had I come upon two women praying for *my livelihood* to be taken away from *me,* in *my workplace,* when *I* had earned a living as an exotic dancer. I am thinking—a fist fight, for beginners, followed by some mementos for any moron trying to undermine me and take my job.

I coughed, and spoke immediately when I saw one of the dancers coming out, and thankfully, the pastor stopped her prayer.

I knew I was called to visit these women, but I knew...we were going about it in the wrong way.

My pastor and I began an internet search of how to effectively minister to strip clubs. I was reminded of a church I attended for a while in Las Vegas that had begun a ministry known as XXX Church. I knew they went to porn conventions in Vegas, and some of the girls who I assumed were from the club, were often sitting in the front row of church.

I was working at our award ribbon business when they called. I called back, and got their voice mail again. In the meantime, my pastor was able to find someone at a national ministry to strippers. They provided information on what this outreach needed to look like.

One of the men who often joined us in the bar ministry told me that he thought his wife would be interested in reaching out to the strip industry. I wasn't sure if he totally understood what we were going to be doing, because his wife, Katie, had sat behind me in church for nearly a year. I couldn't remember ever hearing her speak. She was very demure, lovely, but reserved.

Yet, when I prepared to go for training, others who had an interest were unable to attend, so it was me, Tony, and

Katie in our van. I took this opportunity to get to know Katie better.

The leader of the group was welcoming, however, blunt and to the point. She told us that under no circumstances should we underestimate the gravity of the industry we were entering. She looked at us, and I'm sure she must have thought we were middle aged women with a savior complex. She knew there was no place in the ministry for that egotistical mind set.

I revealed for the first time outside of my pastor and husbands, the truth of my past. Katie asked what the girls would be wearing, having never stepped foot in such a place. The team lead looked her in the face and said, "They are naked. That's why it's called a strip club. If you have a problem hugging naked women, you are going to the wrong place."

As we left, I whispered to Katie "How are you doing?"

She hesitated... "I'm fine so far."

The first club we visited was a "lingerie modeling studio." The ladies there, despite the name, do a whole lot more than model nighties. I had never heard of such a place, even in Las Vegas, known for brothels and strip clubs. I knew that some of the massage studios were actually peddling sex, but we didn't have any lingerie modeling.

The place was located on the second story of an old house. We climbed wooden stairs and rang the bell. Out came a sweet woman who I later learned was the bartender. We had a great conversation about massage therapy licenses, baby showers, (one of the girls who worked there was due any day) and we left. Pretty simple—Katie seemed fine. I was fine. We were all.... fine.

The next place we went was an actual strip club. If I live to be a hundred, I'll never forget that visit. We opened the door, and Cynthia led us inside. She chatted briefly with the door guy, who didn't ask to see our IDs nor charge us. We then turned to enter the club. There, at the end of the runway was a dancer, crouched down spread eagle. The music was loud and thumping a throbbing beat and the lighting was dim.

At this point, I figured I'd lost Katie for good. Nothing I could do about that now though, I figured, so I followed the group leader as she quickly went back to the dressing room.

I gasped. The layout was nearly exactly the same as the dressing room in the first club I where I had danced. Costumes were hung on a bar on the back wall, and a huge mirror on the wall reflected the images of multiple girls doing their makeup. The house mom chatted with our leader, who inquired as to her needs, and explained that some of the gifts were for the dancers' children, and some were for the girls.

I hugged a few girls and helped one with a zipper on a bustier.

And I knew—I was home.

"So, how are you doing Katie?" I asked as we tumbled over one another into the van.

"I'm fine."

"Thank you, Jesus," I whispered to myself.

So it began. We first spent several weeks in prayer before we began to build up resources. We would need gifts and bags. I searched the internet for the cheapest gift bags I could find, and I started searching for inexpensive gift ideas.

Earrings would be great. We could order those in bulk, cheaply. We could make some gifts, so that would save us a lot of money. I found places to get cheap nail art, and friends showed up to stuff the gifts into the bags, pray and write post it notes that said, "Jesus loves working moms," and "You are the daughter of a King." We hoped to keep the cost of the outreach to no more than $100 per month; something I often laugh at that today.

We decided to launch in February—the month we celebrate love! Our first gifts were candy and hearts. I was told to choose double the number of clubs we hoped to enter, because surely, we would be turned down at half of those.

Scrolling through the internet, I learned quickly that the industry was much bigger than I thought. I expected to find about 25 clubs, but I quickly counted over a 100. Where to begin? We chose ten clubs, assuming we could serve five. We still didn't have a name, and you need a name to have a website. Without a site, how could the ladies connect with us if they reached out to us?

We needed something memorable, something that worked both for the industry, speaking to the women there, and to our hope to point the ladies to the source of true freedom, Jesus. And then, while scrolling through the local clubs, God put the name in my heart: Xpose Hope.

When I was in the life, I exposed myself for money, power, and attention. Hope. It's what I want to show the "X" rated industry was hope. In this ministry I would "Xpose Hope" to them.

And so we began. A few bags, three women and a male driver, carrying light and delivering love to the darkness.

We began visiting Club Skinn after a girl-on-girl stabbing that resulted in the murder of one of the dancers. We visited and offered counseling services, as well as prayer. We had been visiting the club for about six months, when we entered one night to face threats and accusations coming from one of the dancers. "Tell those church women to leave! They don't really like us. No church likes strippers or drunks."

What a welcome to a club! The bouncer winced and motioned for us to ignore her, and come on in. When you make the bouncer wince, you have some attitude.

This dancer had some attitude. The rest of the team began to hand gifts to the ladies who wanted to see us, but I couldn't help but reach out to Tiffany. "Why do you think we come here every month, if we don't love you?"

"I don't know, but you church people are haters. I've been to four pastors and none of them will marry me and my fiancé when they find out what I do for work. So, I don't need you, and I don't need no stinkin' church." She spit at me, and tossed a chair my direction. It missed me, but she then attempted to "get physical" and not like Olivia

Newton John, but she was held back by some of the other dancers.

"I'll marry you...I will do the ceremony."

The words just flew out of my mouth. I had no idea where they came from that night, but now, I realize it was God working through me.

"You will?" She calmed down and began to talk to me, sobbing about how all she wanted to do was marry the man she loved, but church after church had refused. She felt alone, despised and unwanted. I had been there myself, so my heart went out to her.

I gave her a hug, and a gift. "Call me anytime, my card is in there."

When we piled into the van, my team asked, "Betty...what have you done?"

"Don't worry. She won't remember me in the morning."

My phone rang at nine a.m. the next morning. "Some women came to our club last night. My name is Tiffany. Will you really marry my fiancé and me?"

I had to scramble at that point. I needed an ordination—and fast. A church we had been involved with had offered to ordain me, and suggested that it might come in handy. But I didn't consider myself worthy of an ordination unless I had a full degree.

But now, I had no choice. I had to make good on my offer. I phoned the pastor and accepted his kind offer.

Not only was my family present, but I invited Tiffany down to join the ceremony. The amazing pastor who provided the ordination explained to the audience that the title of pastor is a calling. Those who are called cannot deny it, and they do not need any human to endorse it. He explained that what we were doing was formalizing what the voice of God had provided for decades ago.

40 years after my original call, I was finally ordained, Pastor Betty.

God has used that ordination multiple times to help me enter jails, hospitals, and officiate funerals. But the greatest blessing was that I was also able to baptize Tiffany on the day that we assisted as she had her criminal record expunged. I now call this beautiful woman my sister in Christ and friend.

I later learned that her husband was a gang member, and the friend of a an infamous local pimp. Before joining the life, he was a pastor's son. He requested that I provide communion and prayer at the ceremony. God can work through anyone!

Beginning the executive director of a ministry does not change the truth that our journey here on earth is going to take some twists and turns. We can't always see what is happening around the corner.

I was busy organizing the items for our annual event when the news came across my phone. The governor had declared that our state was going into quarantine in an attempt to contain the COVID 19 virus. The date of the closure would be three days *prior* to the Xpose Hope fundraising event.

I sat on the couch, put my head in my hands, and wept.

Five years. I had been at this for five years. I had sold my ribbon business when the organization became too much to handle while working. We had exhausted our retirement account as we built the donor base. This was the year that I had targeted to be our crossover year, going from barely existing to becoming a financially-sustaining ministry. I had sold enough seats to our annual event to ensure we'd get some larger donors to begin monthly contributions. Two of ladies were slated to speak about their experience in the life. Food had been donated. We were ready.

And now, that was over. And worse, what was going to happen to our friends in the clubs and on 82nd Street?

The calls began the day of the shutdown. They were horrific calls. Stories of abuse. Stories of trying to find baby food, diapers, and toilet paper. The shelves were empty. There were no back up supplies. Foodbanks were running dry. I listened, and I did a lot of praying and crying.

There had never in the history of the world been a time when "the oldest profession in the world" was shut down. Never.

I was certain, at that moment, Xpose Hope was done. How can you sustain an organization that requires personal interaction for fundraising when your only link to the outside world is a computer? I was crying to my mentor when she put me back in my place. Her pep-talk reeled me back in. "Get on Facebook, and start telling those stories. Tell people about the girls who need food. Talk about the ones thrown out by their boyfriends or pimps. Be the voice for those who have nowhere to go."

And so, I did. I cried my heart out to my Facebook audience. And then, it happened. The miracles began. Diapers, formula, and baby food began to show up on our doorstep. A giant box of toilet paper was donated. And God began to rain money into our social media funding mechanisms.

One by one we served our callers, providing diapers from the stash of a mother who had purchased extra, food from the local Walmart, and housing ladies as far away as Eugene. Our volunteers began to take mentoring classes, and suddenly, we were mentoring more ladies than we had ever served at one time.

When I thought it was over, God said, "I'm here to hold you!"

Xpose Hope has grown exponentially. Beginning with three volunteers, (at this writing) we have expanded to four teams in the Portland Metro area, one in Bend, a presence in Salem and Vancouver, the Tri Cities area of Oregon/Washington, Great Falls, Montana and a team in Pasco County, Florida. We not only visit the strip clubs where women dance, but also drag queens and male strip clubs. We frequent the high prostitution areas, and we work with other agencies to walk beside their clients who come from the life.

The church we began in later chose not to welcome women from the life into their fold, so I was forced again, to learn something new. I poured over manuals explaining how to begin a 501©3 nonprofit, and I filed the paperwork to create our own ministry. Later, my ministry chose to ordain me as pastor, so that I would never again have to search for a church that believed strongly enough in my mission.

We have connected with multiple churches, nonprofits and businesses, locking arms to create a safety net for those who are often shunned by society, and some who have been sold by their own families. We assist the business community by creating advertising avenues, and connection to community, so that everyone feels valued.

Xpose Hope began with one broken woman, who felt she would never belong in polite society, or in the house of a holy God. But, that woman wanted to reach other broken women. A woman who realized that although her life faced mountains of grief and hardships, and the journey was long, she had always been held by the One who created her. He had never quit loving her, would never abandon her and assured her that chapters to her story had yet to be written.

If you are reading this book, and you are questioning your value, please know that above all, you were created by a God who loves you. You are not a mistake. You are not an accident. *He* created you to be just who you are. He has never left you. He is always waiting for you, to let you know that He cares and is eager to have a relationship with you.

Know that your life has value. You belong here even when you feel out of place. You were created with a purpose even if you haven't discovered it yet. You are greatly loved, though sometimes you don't see that in yourself. It is intrinsic to who we are and who we were created to be.

Few would look at me on the street and say, "There is a woman who has a purpose. She is powerful." But this I know—nothing in my life was wasted. Every hurt was used for a purpose, and everything that others hoped would harm me, made me stronger.

Your story is not over. There may be mountains to climb, and you may have a curve ahead blocking your view. But, hope. Trust. Courage. You have other chapters yet to be written.

Isn't time to give the pen to God?

Epilogue

In this section, I hope to introduce you to just a few of the clients whose lives we shared, even if for a brief moment.

She was hanging out the back door of the club, wearing very little, and looking annoyed with us. She saw our team getting into the van and screamed at us, "So you know, I'm going to use the paper in this book to smoke my weed!"

We prayed a lot over those Bibles—special Bibles with stories of strippers who had come out of the life, sandwiched between sections of the Gospel of John. I hoped that those seeds found their way to good soil, planted deep, and I prayed that the seeds, even if dormant for a season would be resting safe and that others would come and water it.

I never saw that young woman again. But I know that God's Word never returns void. It's okay with me that she was angry with us. I too was angry at the church, once upon a time.

———

"I used to go to church." A statuesque, stunningly beautiful young woman announced. She appeared so elegant and self-assured, and reminded me of a large, wild African lion. "But then I couldn't take the bus 3 hours to my old church where people accepted me. So, I tried some churches down here. They wouldn't let me sing."

Unfortunately, we hear many renditions of this same story. Because of their "sinful lifestyles," our ladies are often turned away from any type of service in the church, no matter how small. While accepting that sin is wrong, loving people is the job of the church. I doubt that many, if any churches inquire as to the sins of every singer, musician, nursery worker, janitor, usher or the greeter at the door.

We took Nakeesha to church that Sunday. She brought her child, and she went up to the microphone for testimony time. She poured out her heart and then captivated us with the most beautiful rendition of a gospel hymn I've ever heard. Such a wonderful witness! I realized right there, that the Spirit moves in our ladies, and that He was whispering to them all the time. There were seeds of faith within many who took to the stages in dark places, and it was our job to water those seeds as ambassadors of Christ's love.

———————

The call began, "Hi, my name is Margo. I grew up in Hillsboro, Oregon. My father put me on the street to earn my own way at 12 years old. He was my pimp. When I got old enough to leave him, I found another pimp. I have had four children, and the state took them all. Now, I'm pregnant again, and I'm back in Hillsboro. I don't know where to go, and I have Covid."

Thankfully, at my chamber meeting just that week, it had been mentioned that Hillsboro had Covid housing available for anyone who wasn't housed who tested positive. We were able to find housing, food and medical care for Margo. Her baby was born drug free.

———————

Sadie's family didn't know she had been trafficked. She stood on the stage, with her family present, unsure why she was up there. "My family is going to be very shocked, but I am an Xpose Hope lady. I am a victim of trafficking."

She wanted out, and shortly after we took her from the arms of her pimp, she discovered she was pregnant. She was devastated. Everything seemed against her, first her background, then her lack of employable skills, and now, pregnancy.

Her hope was to become a nurse, and she quickly found appropriate work and began school. Step by step, she has changed her life, and the life of her child.

———

Our relationship with Rosa began in a search. Rosa was a transgendered prostitute who was reported missing when calls from mom went unanswered. Xpose Hope printed fliers and posted them in every club that would allow them, we each had a photo on our phone.

I took dozens of calls from mom, who cried and begged me to talk to God and plead for the healthy return of her child. I did.

When the body was found, a family and community was destroyed. I stood on the podium, to give the eulogy, praying that God would give me the right words to tell a community that by and large, feels unwanted by the world. I would later pray for Rosa's father as he was dying, and do the eulogy for her stepfather, a great man of God and a pillar in the recovery community.

Few days go by that I don't think of Rosa. Every time I post the "Bad DateLine" for our prostitute friends, so that they can stay safe, I pray that I will never say goodbye to someone again, murdered for being who they believed themselves to be...taken from their families too soon.

———

Later that night, Rosa attended a church concert, and

When we entered the club, one of the ladies asked for an extra t-shirt. I explained that we had limited numbers, so she said "Okay, I will give mine to my aunt."

"Why would your aunt want a shirt?"

"Because her daughter is the one that was stabbed. She keeps her room just as it was the last time she walked out of it. She keeps one of every gift you give to us, on the dresser."

With tears, I handed her the cotton tee, printed with the words "Jesus Loves Strippers." It was a moment that is forever etched in my mind. What a blessing.

The true miracle happened when the young woman asked me, "Are you visiting the girl who did this in jail?"

"We are trying to." I had to be honest. We love the victim, and we love the perpetrator. God came to heal us all.

"Please give her a message from us. We hear she is suicidal due to her sentencing. Please tell her that Jesus loves her. Tell her that we forgive her."

Who would have thought, we'd find the love of Jesus in a strip club?

About Betty

Betty Campbell is a *former* writer, fashion editor and contributing editor, as well as a successful entrepreneur.

Currently, she is the founder and executive director of Xpose Hope, a nonprofit that reaches trafficked persons and those in adult entertainment. Xpose Hope is currently operating in four states.

Connect with Betty:

www.BettyLCampbell.com
www.xposehope.com
www.facebook.com/AuthorBettyCampbell
www.linkedin.com/in/betty-campbell-22677044
www.instagram.com/bettycampbellauthor